The Author

Dexter and Karen with
my best wishes.

Jack Routledge

15 Aug. 03.

TITLE EXPLANATION

Lancaster; a four engine heavy bomber flown by the Royal Air Force and other Commonwealth air forces over Europe during the Second World War.

Lanyard: a white braided rope worn by members of the Royal Canadian Mounted Police about their necks and attached to their revolvers. During the period covered in this book, the *lanyard* was worn on the working and dress uniform. It is now worn only on the dress uniform.

LANCASTERS AND LANYARDS

MEMOIRS

OF

CHIEF SUPERINTENDENT

JACK DENISON ROUTLEDGE D.F.C.

ROYAL CANADIAN MOUNTED POLICE (RETIRED)

Printed in Victoria, Canada

National Library of Canada Cataloguing in Publication Data

Routledge, Jack, 1924-
    Lancasters and lanyards : memoirs of Chief Superin-
tendent Jack Denison Routledge (D.F.C.) Royal Canadian
Mounted Police
(Retired) / written by Jack Routledge ; edited by Shirley
Campbell.
ISBN 1-4120-0099-8
    1. Routledge, Jack, 1924- 2. Royal Canadian Mounted
Police--Biography. 3. World War, 1939-1945--Aerial opera-
tions, British--Personal narratives, Canadian. I.
Campbell, Shirley, 1937- II. Title.
HV7911.R68A3 2003   363.2'092   C2003-901581-5

TRAFFORD

This book was published *on-demand* in cooperation with Trafford Publishing.
On-demand publishing is a unique process and service of making a book available for retail sale to the public taking advantage of on-demand manufacturing and Internet marketing.
On-demand publishing includes promotions, retail sales, manufacturing, order fulfilment, accounting and collecting royalties on behalf of the author.

Suite 6E, 2333 Government St., Victoria, B.C. V8T 4P4, CANADA
Phone   250-383-6864   Toll-free   1-888-232-4444 (Canada & US)
Fax   250-383-6804   E-mail   sales@trafford.com
Web site   www.trafford.com   TRAFFORD PUBLISHING IS A DIVISION OF TRAFFORD HOLDINGS LTD.
Trafford Catalogue #03-0462   www.trafford.com/robots/03-0462.html

10   9   8   7   6   5   4   3   2

Pen and Ink Artwork by Lois Mollard

'Through Adversity to the Stars'

Nothing in this world came without cost. We as Canadians should be forever thankful for the life as we know it now. Our constant vigilance is required to defend Canada, it's freedoms, rights, and privileges obtained by great sacrifice.

Jack D. Routledge

PERSONAL ACKNOWLEDGEMENTS

I wish to express my particular appreciation to the following people for their assistance and support in composing this document:

My wife, Margaret, daughter Patricia and son Bruce along with friends, have asked me to put into writing what transpired during my life so it can be shared by them and others.

Our very dear friends Dr. Hugh Clarke and his wife Anne who aided my work-in-progress. Anne gave me confidence in working a computer and rescued me from each seemingly insurmountable problem. Hugh kindly accepted the arduous duty of proof-reading my first manuscript, not the easiest of tasks, as my spelling and grammar could not be considered as the best.

Renée Mackenzie, our next-door neighbour, would rush to rescue me from self-inflicted computer frustrations. Also, her husband, Captain Ian Mackenzie (Marine), who volunteered to give the entire manuscript a another proof-reading and advice.

My two friends, Don Weixl and Chris Walsh, for their patient assistance in unlocking other computer problems over the years

During the past three years, a great deal of research was needed to authenticate statements made in my memoirs and to search for companies or individuals to obtain their permission to publish their works. I corresponded with persons and organizations here in Canada and in England. The Administrator for DMZee Marketing Limited, England, gracefully volunteered to assist me in my quest.

Martin Middlebrook and Chris Everett of England made an exhaustive study and co-authored the book, *The*

Bomber Command War Diaries, An Operational Reference Book: 1939 to 1945, published by the Penguin Group in 1985 and 1990. I am grateful for Martin Middlebrook's permission to quote from this publication. Mr Middlebrook, a fellow of the Royal Historical Society, is also the author of *The Berlin Raids, The Nuremberg Raid, Battle of Hamburg* and other Bomber Command activities.

Mr. Gribbon of Gribbon Enterprises of Elmira, Ontario, was extremely helpful in obtaining my operational flying records and other related material of our crew while we were with 405 Squadron (R.C.A.F.) at Gransden Lodge near Cambridge.

The executive of 49 Squadron Association in England, particularly L.J. 'Uncle Will' Hay, rendered assistance in obtaining my operational flying records and other related documents covering my service with 49 Squadron (R.A.F) from the Public Archives, Kew, Richmond, England, and from the 49 Squadron Association. He also devoted a great deal of effort to locating persons and documents for me.

I thank Mr. Steve Vessey of 46, Fiskerton Road, Reepham, Lincolnshire, England, for his diligent search for a photograph of Lancaster PM-M2 over Lincoln. I also thank Group Captain Phil Goodman, Commanding Officer of R.A.F. Station Conningsby and Navigator of the Memorial Lancaster, for his donation of an autographed photo of the Memorial Lancaster.

Dr. John Allin of Grantham, Lincolnshire, gave me historical bits of information and the two photos of our 49 Squadron Lancaster EA-E flying over the English Channel. These pictures had been obtained from Wing Commander Slee, the C.O. of 49 Squadron. Dr. Allin, recently deceased, was the son of Sgt. John Allin R.A.F. mentioned in chapter three of these memoirs.

Book Production Consultants Plc., publishers, granted permission to use "50 Years On," the first fifteen pages of the book by Mr. John Goley and Bill Gunston called *So Many*. See Appendix C. Regrettably John Goley recently died.

The web site of The Air Force Association of Canada was extremely useful in obtaining verification of citations, awards and decorations from an alphabetical list of over 8,000 recipients. This information as shown in Appendix A was compiled by Mr. Hugh Halliday of Orleans, Ontario, under the heading, 'RCAF Personnel-Honours and Awards 1939–1945.' I am most appreciative of his work.

Assistant Commissioner Ed. Witherden (Retired) and Inspector Vern. Williams (Retired) of the Royal Canadian Mounted Police undertook to early proof-read this document and offered constructive suggestions.

Mrs. Simma Holt was a correspondent for the *Vancouver Sun* with whom I became acquainted during my tenure with the investigations of the Sons of Freedom Sect of the Doukhobors. She became one of law enforcement's friends after her in depth study of the religious problem within this group. She authored the book *Terror in the Name of God*, after living within this group of terrorists for many months. This book was an ideal reference.

Permission was received from Larry T. Wright to reproduce the Mine Laying Code Names and the Mine Laying Statistics as they appear in the Web Site and as shown in Appendix B.

I also at this time wish to express my appreciation to Shirley Campbell, B.A. (Hon.), M.A., my editor, for utilizing her wealth of knowledge in bringing this book to the publishing stage.

The last, but by no means the least to be acknowledged, is Assistant Commissioner E.W. Willes (LLB), Royal Canadian Mounted Police (Retired).

Table of Contents

List of Photographs and Illustrations

Forward

I first met Jack Routledge in 1965 when he made periodic visits to my office in Chilliwack B.C. At that time he was in charge of Special 'D' Section of the Royal Canadian Mounted Police. That unit was based in Nelson B.C., but his duties required him to make regular enquiries at the Federal Penitentiary, called Mountain Prison, near Agassiz B.C., where the convicted Sons of Freedom Doukhobors were serving their time. Following his visits to the prison, he briefed my staff and me on the current activities of the Sons of Freedom Sect.

My first impression of Jack Routledge was very favourable. He struck me as sincere, knowledgeable and a dedicated police officer. Later we worked together in the Royal Canadian Mounted Police Headquarters in Ottawa, Ontario. Jack was in charge of the National Crime Intelligence Units of the Force, and during this period I was in daily contact with him and could observe and assess his capabilities first hand. I must say that the experience simply reinforced my first impression of Jack Routledge. He was hard-working, innovative and readily adaptable to change. Our working relationship developed into a close personal friendship that has been sustained over the years.

When reading his memoirs, it occurred to me that the strict and often unhappy discipline he was subjected to as a youngster, coupled with the stressful demands of his war service, aptly schooled him to meet the challenges he faced throughout his career. His narrative chronicles the achievements of a dedicated public servant. His career played out in relative anonymity; therefore, it is only fitting that he has recorded his life story.

I found his account of his war service fascinating and I commend his memoirs to all who are interested in the achievements of a dedicated Canadian who served his country with dedication in both war and peace.

Assistant Commissioner E.W.Willes, LLB,
Royal Canadian Mounted police (Retired)

Introduction

My memoirs will highlight four distinct periods. The first tells of my family and my difficult childhood to age sixteen when I signed up in 1940 with the Royal Canadian Air Force. The second period is my wartime service from 1940 to 1945. During that period, I flew as a rear gunner in four-engine Lancaster bombers with the Royal Air Force in England and survived unscathed. My wartime experiences had a profound effect on my life and they continue to do so now.

After several years of dislocation following my discharge, I enlisted into the British Columbia Provincial Police in 1949 to 1950 and eventually served with the Royal Canadian Mounted Police from 1950 to 1979. I have included some of the anxious moments and humorous incidents.

Finally, I relate something of the occurrences of my five years from 1979 to 1984 as chairman of the Driver Control Board for the province of Alberta.

Since my retirement in 1984, I have had time to savour my experience and mull over its meaning. The number of World War Two veterans is diminishing, and I am happy to share what I remember of those days. My experiences in the police, which classed as quasi-military, may contribute to an understanding of these branches of service. I hope so.

I wish to emphasize that each of the incidents that I have included is based entirely on fact and first hand knowledge. Nor have I written about any situation that could not be recalled without some degree of clarity and in most instances, support. In some situations I have named a person, group or organization and the comments may appear derogatory. My intention has been neither to be malicious nor to cause embarrassment or harm. If I have offended in any way, I offer my sincere apologies.

All quotations with respect to my career in the Royal Canadian Air Force from 1940 to 1945 are fully supported by my flying log book, plus archival records obtained from 49 Squadron and 405 Squadron as maintained by the Public Records Office, Kew, Richmond, Surrey, England. Further, many of the statistics were obtained from writings by Martin Middlebrook of England, a noted and respected historian and author on Royal Air Force Bomber Command History and their Operations during the Second World War.

Verification of statements about my police service and court cases can also be obtained from service files of the Royal Canadian Mounted Police. The same holds true regarding the various investigations mentioned. They are fully supported by R.C.M. Police records, the Supreme Court of British Columbia, the Supreme Court of Ontario and B. C. Provincial Court documents.

There are four symbols, the Maple Leaf flag of Canada, the Royal Canadian Air Force flag, the crest of the R.C.A.F. and the crest of the Royal Canadian Mounted Police. I have served all my life at one time or another under one or more of these symbols for which I am extremely proud as they had and still have a profound effect on me. I would like to take a few moments and explain their significance.

During the war Canada did not have a distinct flag to wave; we had the 'Red Ensign' of Britain but we still served Canada with pride. After a great deal of debate in our parliament and input from the public on a design, the flag was replaced on February 15th, 1965, with the Red Maple Leaf, which is distinctly Canadian.

The Royal Canadian Air Force flag was inherited from the Royal Air Force of England. This flag has a blue background with the Union Jack in the upper left corner but the roundel in the right centre has a Red Maple Leaf inserted where normally a red dot would be shown.

The air force crest is distinctly Canadian also. The crest has the Queen's Crown, below which is a belt forming a circle and a blue centre with an eagle imposed across the belt. Written on the belt is the Latin motto 'Per Ardua ad Astra' meaning 'Through Adversity to the Stars'. A banner is affixed to the lower portion on which 'Royal Canadian Air Force' is inscribed.

The crest of the Royal Canadian Mounted Police has the Queen's Crown surmounting a belt surrounding a buffalo head. On the belt is inscribed 'Maintiens le Droit' which translated means 'Maintain the Right.' It in turn is encircled with leaves. A banner on the bottom reads 'Royal Canadian Mounted Police.'

As you will read, 'Through Adversity to the Stars' and 'Maintain the Right' have played an important part of my life and continue to this day to do so.

Any expression of opinion in this book is entirely that of the author.

Chapter 1

My Earlier Conflicts

1924 to 1940

The war medal of my paternal grandfather Thomas Routledge came into my possession in 1998 and now hangs by my own. He was awarded this medal for his volunteer service in 1866 with the Canadian Militia during the Fenian Raids. My own medals were awarded me for service in World War Two while serving in the Royal Canadian Air Force from 1940 to 1945. The engraving on the medal gives his name and says he was a gunner- many years later I too became a gunner but in an aircraft.

I do believe my grandfather was born in Carlisle on the English-Scottish border and immigrated to Canada. Sometime prior to Confederation, he served with the militia when Canada was confronted with an armed invasion from the United States by bands of Fenians. The Fenians were Irish Americans who disliked England on principle and more especially because of England's sympathy with the Southern Confederacy, which had recently lost to the Northern Unionists in the American Civil War. To punish England, the Fenians attacked her colony along the border in eastern Canada, and the Militia was successful in repelling them. Nearly eighty years later, I was in England involved in a similar task against Nazism.

My grandfather became a locomotive engineer with the Canadian Pacific Railway (C.P.R.). My father, Percival Harold Routledge, was born in London, Ontario, on Christmas Day, 1892. Despite the auspices, I did not find my father the prince of peace. His sister Stella married a Wilfred Wilson who eventually became a conductor on the C.P.R. at Moosejaw, Saskatchewan. Aunt Stella fell heir to her father's medal and passed it on to her daughter Bessie Don, who passed it on to me. I have no idea why the medal was not passed to my father. As the only son he would seem to be the likely recipient, but apparently not.

Dad grew up in London, Ontario, and also worked for the C.P.R. He then terminated his employment and moved to Regina, Saskatchewan, where he rejoined the firm. It was here he met my mother, Ethel Mary Dennison, born in Brantford, Ontario, in 1898. As her parents were long deceased when I came on the scene and as a youngster, I failed to ask any pertinent questions about them. Very early in the century my mother's parents moved to Qu'Appelle, Saskatchewan, to farm. She told us of the harsh life they had to endure in the early days, especially for a large family for, unlike my dad, she had many brothers and sisters, some of whom I have met. There was Ormand, Ethan, Bessie, and Viola, and I think another brother and several more sisters. When mother went to Regina to work as a secretary for one of the wheat companies there, she met and married Dad. The C.P.R. transferred him to Estevan, Saskatchewan, where he worked as a fireman for several years. My eldest sibling, Kathleen was born here. About 1920 my father left the C.P.R. and moved to Mission, British Columbia. He got a job as a mechanic with a Mr. Joe Hargitt. He and mom lived above the garage and it was here that my brother Jim was born on September 2nd, 1922.

Father eventually bought some lots at the east end of Main Street and built his own garage which he called Routledge Motors. We rented a home from a Robert Wardrop, three lots up the hill from the garage, and it was in this house I was born on March 30th, 1924. Eventually my parents built a house next to the garage where I lived until I left to join the Royal Canadian Air Force in 1940. This house is still standing and has been renovated into offices and is called the Rutledge House. The misspelling of the name was an error by the owner, and after some discussion she wasn't about to change it because of the cost.

Mission is located forty-three miles east of Vancouver on the north side of the Fraser River and on the main transcontinental line of the Canadian Pacific Railway. Population at this time was about 2000 people who were employed mainly in the dairy, fruit farming and lumber business. Japanese Canadians operated the majority of the fruit farms. Many Japanese children attended school, and then most of them would go to their own Japanese School, located near the fairgrounds, after the regular public school hours. The Catholic Church maintained a large residential school for First Nations children, located on a bench overlooking the Fraser River a mile east of town. It was from this school that the village derived its name of Mission. Lifestyle in our village was, I imagine, no different from other Canadian small towns, somewhat laid back.

The depression years caused serious economic problems throughout the country. Every person and business had to cut expenses as money became extremely scarce. My father would take sacks of wheat and oats or bales of straw, meat or eggs from people for payment of their accounts. In some instances people were given credit for repairs and would leave town without settling their bill. After the war my father spent a lot of time tracking them down and went personally to collect the money, usually successfully.

My father was a tough businessman, and yet was compassionate when it came to dealing with people who were hard-working but having great difficulty making ends meet. A mechanic for my father by the name of Barnett became paraplegic after a car fell on him. This injury happened years before the existence of a Workmen's Compensation Board, so my father paid this man for many years in order that the family could survive.

Theo Kramer was my father's bookkeeper. He lived with his wife Phyllis, son Kenneth and daughter Lydia in a bungalow at the top of the hill on Stave Lake Road. This house was on my paper route and I recall vividly a small girl named Lydia meeting me and taking in the paper. In later years after the war, Lydia married a local boy named Ken Hollas, who was by this time a member of the Royal

Canadian Mounted Police. Since my post-war career was with the R.C.M.P., our paths crossed several times in Nelson, B.C., then Ottawa, Ontario, and later in Edmonton, Alberta. We still maintain contact to this date.

Our family was growing larger. Dorothea and Thomas now brought the children count to five. I was the middle child, a very unenviable position, neither old enough nor young enough, and always in trouble. There were times I was punished for mischief I did do, and there were times I was punished for things I took no part in. When I say punished, I mean severely. Father, being a garage owner, did not strap us with a belt but with a length of car brake lining. It was kept in a drawer in the kitchen and he used it regularly. One day my brother Jim suggested we throw the strap into the coal and wood stove. I agreed and the deed was done. Some days later our father got into a terrible rage over something we had done or not done. He went to the drawer for the strap and found it was gone. His rage went up about forty decibels. Our younger sister Dorothea told him what we had done with the strap and he became so worked up that he chased me through the house. He caught me at the top of the basement stairs, gave me a boot on the backside and I tumbled twelve steps to the basement floor. Needless to say, I was crying and ended up with some scrapes and bruises. This time my mother really lit into him with a tongue-lashing.

Our father was quite a heavy drinker. At times my mother would send me to the garage to tell him his supper was ready. I would look through the office and the cars in the garage and several times found him sleeping in the back seat of one of them. I would tell my mother where he was and she would tell us to sit down and have our supper without him. He had a room in the back of the garage, which was referred to as his snake room, where he and his drinking friends would quickly consume a bottle of whisky. The more he drank the more belligerent he became. I can honestly say, however, I never saw him abuse my mother.

One Christmas when Jim and I were about twelve and ten years old, my father gave us each a pair of boxing gloves. When he and his cronies were drinking, he would call Jim and me to put on the boxing gloves and come to the snake pit, where we would be ordered to entertain them with a boxing match. I was not a fighter so inevitably I ended up the loser and always with a terrible headache. My lack of enthusiasm on these occasions did not endear me to my father, as I felt he thought I was a weakling. I guess I should have treated the gloves the same as the brake lining strap. I hated those gloves then and I still detest anything related to boxing.

Among the many fine families in Mission, social activities were the main form of entertainment. Ted Calvert, Forest Ranger for the B.C. Forest Service, his wife Peggy, son Tom and daughter Margaret moved from Squamish to Mission in 1932. My brother Jim and their son Tom were in the same grade, Margaret was in grade 1 and I was in Grade 2. Alec and John Stuart, sons of Forbes and Bea Stuart, lived across the street from us; Alec was in Jim's class and John was in mine. Then there was Spud Rose, later known by his proper name of Mark, who shared the same grade with me until I enlisted. Other boyhood friends were John Wardrop from next door, Bill and Ted McIntyre, sons of the local doctor, Walker MacCallum, son of a local hardware store owner, and many more school chums who remained friends over the years. Tragically, Ted McIntyre and John Wardrop were killed in the air force during the war in flying accidents, Ted in Alberta and John at Cottesmore in England.

I had a paper route for five years; the money I earned enabled me to buy a bicycle. After my paper route and on week-ends, I was supposed to pump gasoline and fix flat tires at the garage. I was never permitted to participate in the sports that went on in my pal John Stuart's yard, directly across the street from the garage. Accordingly, I would come home from delivering papers and then take off out the door looking for my buddies. It would always lead to a confrontation with my father, as he expected me at the garage. My favourite excuse was that I forgot. My father knew better, and despite the consequences I would try it again and again. In retrospect, I suppose I pushed his patience to the limit.

However, there were times when we could go out and get into mischief. The C.P.R. station was a great place for activity in the evenings, particularly in the summer months. Bats would dive under the station overhang when feeding on mosquitoes. We would swing sweaters or whatever at them but always missed. We then found an old corn broom and used it with pretty good accuracy. Having stunned the bats, we would then place them in a paper bag and take them to the alley behind the movie theatre, where the theatre's fire escape doors would be open for cooling, there being no air conditioning in those days. While the film was being shown, we would sneak into the darkened room and shake the bats out of the bag. They would take to wing across the projection light and into the screen, causing absolute bedlam among the patrons. I think Sam Bannister, the theatre owner, thought the bats flew in the open doors on their own.

Our attendance at the train station in the evenings brought about rewards from an unexpected source. The eastbound transcontinental trains from Vancouver used to stop in Mission to take on water, mail, express and passengers. During this interval the chef on one dining car would lean on the Dutch door to watch the activities at the station and we struck up a conversation with him. As the train was heading east, we would not see him again for about a week or ten days, and then one day there he would be. He would talk to us for a bit, look up and down the length of the train to be sure nobody was watching, then call us over and hand us a bag, telling us to keep it level. We would go up on the bank above the station and open the bag to find a hot pie right out of the oven. Needless to say, we four or five young ruffians consumed it. We quickly established the chef's schedule, and like the proverbial sea gulls we were at the station looking for our hand-out. He never let us down.

The train station in fact, was a continual source of creative entertainment. When the first passenger train of the evening arrived to take on water, the engineer would grease all the drive rods with a special grease gun. The gun used rods of grease, and when the grease rod got low, the engineer would knock the left-over onto the ground and install a new one. Twenty minutes after this train left, the second section would arrive, and this train crew would go through the same procedures. We collected these lumps of grease from the first train and placed them on the tracks where we thought the drive wheels of the second section would stop. Then we watched the fun. As the engineer slowly opened the throttle to make a smooth start with his fifteen heavy passenger cars, there was no movement. The engine would just sit and slip on the rails, belching great clouds of smoke and steam. He would put it in reverse, and the same thing would happen. He would apply sand with no results. After many attempts of forward and reverse, he would finally break loose from the greasy track. The perplexed look on the engineer's face was priceless. So even though we had no money, we made our own live entertainment at the expense of the C.P.R. and the local theatre.

We kids grew up with a black and white Alsatian dog named Rinty. Wherever Jim or I went, this dog was the third person. He would go to school with us, return home until lunch time, then come back and be waiting for us at the school door. He would repeat this same procedure at the end of the school day. At night he was put in the garage next door as a watchdog, and he was very good, although he got himself into trouble with my father once in a while. On these occasions when being taken to his post, he would bolt for freedom because he had detected a female dog in heat. At times he was gone two or three days, but he would eventually return and all would be forgiven.

Our home was situated within a block of the railway tracks. Every westbound freight train stopped at the railway crossing and took on water, as this was the last stop before Vancouver. As the depression worsened, every train carried more and more hoboes. These poor souls would get off the train in Mission to avoid the C.P.R. Police waiting for them in Vancouver. Many of them came to the door looking for work of any description and would accept a meal as payment. My mother would have them split wood or do any other outside chore and give them a meal. Rinty did not like these strangers so it was panic stations to get him inside the house before they reached the gate.

Care of the environment was not high on our priority list during the 1930s. All of Mission's garbage was trucked down to the bank of the Fraser River adjacent to the C.P.Railway bridge and dumped over the bank into the water. The location became a haven for hundreds of rats. Our dog hated rats and he would go to no end to catch one and kill it. The dump was honeycombed with holes and passages dug by the rats. A group of us would take our fishing lines, bait the hook with a little meat, shake the hook down one of the holes and wait. Shortly the line would tug and we would yank a rat out and beat it with sticks or turn the dog loose. Our activities did not significantly reduce the rat population, but it did provide us with a rather sadistic sport.

When this wonderful dog got too old and had to be put down, the whole family was devastated, particularly Jim and I. My father then bought a Great Dane pup, a move that upset mother as the dog was very difficult to control. When he got into the house he would romp from room to room, whacking his long thin tail against sharp corners of the French doors, causing it to bleed, and spraying the walls and ceiling with blood. When he was put in the garage at night as a watchdog, all he did was howl continuously, much to the concern of the neighbours. This poor dog did not last long; he ran onto the road in front of the house and was killed by a passing car.

At this time on my paper route I had befriended a Cocker spaniel named Spud owned by a Mr. Thom, operator of the local creamery. When his neighbour Mr. Chell accused the dog of killing his chickens, Mr. Thom offered him to me.

I quickly accepted. When I took him home I was in serious trouble with both parents; however, I managed to weather the storm and was allowed to keep him. We also had chickens, but I did not reveal this aspect of Spud's history. To my surprise he paid no attention to our birds, and when I told Mr. Thom he expressed no surprise, and I began to think the chicken story was for my benefit.

This spaniel turned out to be the greatest four-footed fisherman a person ever saw. During the spawning season the salmon would be in the shallow pools in the Stave River below the Ruskin Dam. I would put the dog in the paper carrier on my bicycle and along with other kids go fishing in the river. This dog would spend the whole time leaping into the pools and attempting to grab the fish. Most of the time he would fail, but once in a while he would succeed. The big salmon would pull him under and he would come to the surface sputtering and panting, then be off after another one.

When I enlisted in the air force, Spud took up with my younger brother Tom, who liked fishing in the Fraser River. One day Tom caught a sturgeon two feet long and kept it although the legal length was three feet. He brought it home and convinced mother to let him put it in a bathtub of water. Unfortunately, the bathroom door was left open and Spud saw the fish. He leaped in and grabbed it by the back. A sturgeon's back conceals large spikes which pierced his mouth; that in turn made him more determined to hang on, and the ensuing battle caused water and blood to be splattered everywhere. Mother immediately revoked her permission to keep the fish. It was returned to the river.

When Jim and I were about nine and seven years old, my mother thought we had a talent in music and that it should be pursued. She sent us to John Stobbs, a local music teacher, to become proficient on the violin. We had great difficulty in holding the violin, plus the bow, let alone understanding music. Once a week we would go through the motions at Stobbs' house, and I am sure he suffered great anguish over the lack of progress. Although we told our mother we did not like the violin, she insisted until finally John Stobbs told her there was no hope for either of us. I tell you, we were two happy kids.

Our musical adventures did not end there. A wonderful man by the name of Alfred Hills, occupation painter, started a band under the auspices of the United Church. He was taking kids whether they had talent or not. He undertook to teach those with no musical training, and bring along those who did. Both of the Routledge brats joined, mainly because all our buddies had. Jim was on the coronet and I on the trumpet. I couldn't carry a note even if it was in a suitcase.

The band grew close to thirty members. Believe it or not, we did quite well. The non-talented ones were brought along by Mr. Hills as well as other more experienced members like Mark (Spud) Rose. We performed proudly at various community functions in our light and dark blue uniforms. How talented I had become was a very large question in my mind. I used to see Mr. Hill grimace and look at me when we were practising. The experience though was good for all of us. The sincerity and hard work put into this effort by our conductor was fantastic. Even at this late period in our lives, former band members still like to reminisce about their experiences in the band.

My parents used to have the odd social gathering with the Calvert family. One Christmas they were at our house and I recall the adults trying to get me to kiss Margaret Calvert under the mistletoe. I was twelve years old and Margaret was eleven, and I found the whole prospect embarrassing and refused. Jim, then fourteen, did kiss Margaret to the delight of the adults, but I ran and hid. I did not know then that one day we would marry.

One winter evening about 1937, the four Routledge children were invited to the Calvert house for an evening with a new game called Monopoly. While we were there, it started to snow and then became freezing rain. Little did we realize how bad the weather was until it was time to go home. We lived only three blocks away, but after many phone calls to parents, Jim and I went home leaving Dorothea and Tom overnight in the care of the Calverts. This ice storm went on all night and by morning there was no power and trees and poles were down. The roads were not fit to drive on and the town was in a terrible mess. The ice storm absolutely crippled the Fraser Valley. Power was not restored for a week, highways were closed, and trains did not run for four days. Eventually the weather warmed and the ice disappeared, but the clean-up was a tremendous effort that took many months.

Building model aircraft was a hobby I very much enjoyed, and I suppose it eventually led to my interest in flying. The aircraft were made of balsa wood and rice paper and powered by an elastic band. I had built dozens of them over the years. Pioneer Motors across the street from my father's garage was operated by Lou Hudson, who had his private pilot's licence. Once a month he would go to Vancouver and fly from the Sea Island Airport in a rented Piper Cub aeroplane. Even though Lou was in competition with my father, he would sometimes ask me to go with him. Usually his wife and daughter Margaret would travel with him but they did not fly. Lou gave me my first experience at flying and I enjoyed every second. I recall on my last trip to the airport with him, a Hawker Hurricane parked outside the hangar gave us an opportunity for a close look. I must say I was really impressed with this very latest and fastest fighter of the Royal Air Force. Canada had purchased ten or twelve of them. Prior to the war, a Hurricane was flying from Vancouver to Calgary when it ran into foul weather over the Fraser Valley near Mission and became lost. Eventually, the pilot bailed out, but unfortunately both aircraft and he landed on the road that leads to a rural district called Dureau, located several miles northeast of Mission. He was killed and the plane totally demolished. At the outbreak of war, Lou Hudson joined the Commonwealth Air Training Plan as a civilian instructor. He helped train pilots from all over the Commonwealth.

My father was an excellent mechanic and machinist. While in Saskatchewan and employed by the C.P.R., he built a scaled down steam powered locomotive used by the railway. About 1936 he decided to build another steam locomotive modelled after the C.P.R. 'Royal Hudson.' He spent many hours working on it in his workshop in the garage, and of course expected his two older sons to do the same. His philosophy was that every boy should become a mechanic. My brother Jim was inclined this way, but I was not. Even so, I had to clean up the machine shop every week. He thought that by exposing me to the machines, such as, lathes, drill press, etc., I would be inspired and get more involved. The plan didn't work at the time, but other local kids like Tom Calvert jumped at the opportunity and became quite proficient. The engine was finished about 1941 while I was overseas. My father laid tracks in the vacant lot next to the garage and carried passengers for five cents a ride. During the war he collected over five thousand dollars for the Red Cross. After the war he sold his garage business and retired. The engine was sold to Mattocks Farm in Victoria and eventually to a person living in Pennsylvania, U.S.A. His smaller locomotive was left to the family in his will, which in turn was gifted to the Mission Museum where it is on display at the present time along with other items of the Routledge family. After the war I developed an interest in model railroading, not steam driven but electric.

My father had a tow truck and would be called out at all hours of the night. When Jim was fifteen years old, he and I were sent out with the wrecker to accidents. Some of these were quite serious, but Jim and I became adept at pulling cars up steep banks and from other precarious positions. When I turned sixteen, I went for my driver's licence to the Driver Examiner, who conducted his exams in the local B.C. Provincial Police office in Mission. The man in charge of the detachment was Corporal Jack Renner. When my written exam was done, the Examiner announced that he would now take me for the driving test. Corporal Renner responded that he didn't think a test was necessary, as he could vouch for my driving capabilities. No doubt he had seen our antics with the wrecker! With that comment from the local chief of police, I was issued a licence.

Corporal Renner had a very attractive daughter the same age as my brother. Jim, along with about four other fellows, was vying for her attention. I often raised the subject much to his annoyance. One evening he was in the bathroom getting all dolled up and I asked him if he was going out with the two-timer again. He dropped everything and took after me and gave me a beating. Now, that is brotherly love.

The Renners were a very fine family and my parents got to know them quite well as they lived on the opposite side of our block. While I was overseas in England, my mother advised me that Jack Renner was seriously ill with cancer. I did something I had never done before. I wrote him a long letter to tell him how things were going in England and also to give him words of encouragement. I then signed the letter as a member of the Dead End Kids of Mission. Mrs. Renner told me after the war that my letter gave her husband the greatest lift, and he would read it to every visitor he had. Jack Renner died about six months later. The fact that he had enjoyed my letter in his final days made me feel good also.

In 1938 my oldest sister Kathleen married Lorne Mitchell of Mission and they moved to Kamloops. Lorne came from a very fine family in Mission and I have often said, if I was going to choose a brother-in-law, I could not have done any better. He was a gentleman and a pleasure to be associated with. They adopted two children and had two more of their own.

School went on as usual, but I was not doing well. Jim was one year ahead of me and failed grade 10, so the next year he was in the same class as I. Togetherness in class did not make our brotherly relationship any closer. As far as he was concerned, I was a nuisance; he was grown up, dating girls and all that stuff, and he didn't need me around.

I was fifteen years old in 1939 when the Second World War started. It really grabbed my interest, and I started following developments closely. I just wanted to fly, so I sent an application to the Royal Navy Fleet Air Arm in England, but they as much as said, 'Grow up and get an education.' I next applied to the Canadian Navy, and they in turn said I was too young, but gave the caveat that if I had an affidavit from my parents saying I was eighteen they would accept me. That answer made me think that if the Navy would accept this document, then the Royal Canadian Air Force would too. I cautiously approached my mother and brought her up to date. She must have discussed it with my father, as his only comment was, 'He has to join up as a mechanic,' but this is not what I wanted to do. The R.C.A.F. recruiting office in Vancouver initially rejected me for air crew as my nasal passages were blocked with cartilage, but if it were surgically removed I was told I would be accepted. I was very careful to advise my parents that because of my medical rejection I was prevented from enlisting for *ground* crew. Accordingly they agreed. The surgery was performed in St. Paul's hospital in Vancouver. At age sixteen, clutching an affidavit that said I was eighteen, I was accepted in the Royal Canadian Air Force as air crew.

Over the years I have pondered the decision my mother made in signing the affidavit. She put her reputation on the line. If this statement had been detected as being untrue, she might have been charged with perjury. I have two theories for why she did it. Firstly, I was such a problem to them both that this was the best route to get me out of the house. Secondly, it was mother's way of getting me away from my father's wrath before something more drastic happened. I am leaning more to the second theory. However, I never approached either of my parents after the war to find out if I was right. Perhaps both theories were rather unpleasant in fact.

What I have said about my father is not meant to be vengeful or vindictive. This is the way he was. He was his own man, with an attitude that every person, particularly his sons, had to be of the same metal. He was not well educated, but extremely intelligent in his own right. He was a master mechanic and a machinist and favoured any person who was of the same mind-set. Unfortunately, I did not qualify and no amount of punishment could make me fit his mould. We never got along even after the war.

What was accomplished in my first sixteen years? I have at times said as a joke, if it hadn't been for the war, I would probably have ended up in gaol. I learned many valuable lessons from my experiences of growing up. Believe me, after December, 1940, I was still growing up and on a very fast learning curve. I was on my own and this experience was either going to kill me or make me smarter. Overall, I think my family upbringing may have played a large part in my future development, and in this process I give some credit to my father. He made me struggle against him in order to become my own man.

Chapter 2

Enlistment

1940 to 1942

Armed with an affidavit affirming my birth date as March 30th, 1922, I hitchhiked to Vancouver and reported to the R.C.A.F. Recruiting Centre in the Post Office Building on the corner of Granville and Hastings Streets. After an all-day session with medical exams and interviews, I was sworn in as a Wireless Operator Air Gunner. I was issued with railway tickets and sleeping and dining car tickets to travel to Number 2 Manning Depot, Brandon, Manitoba. As it was the 22nd of December, I was allowed to return home to prepare for my journey and spend Christmas, then scheduled to leave Mission on the 28th of December.

I was very excited and could hardly contain myself. My father asked me if I had joined as a mechanic and I told him I was a mechanic and a wireless operator. I knew he had no idea that there wasn't such a position in the air force, and my conscience bothered me for a while. My parents and some friends came to the station to see me off to war. I boarded the same eastbound train we used to put grease under the drive wheels, but on this evening the train eased out of the station without any problem. I asked after the chef we had befriended over the years and was advised he was westbound out of Winnipeg at this time. As the train headed into the Fraser Canyon, I looked forward to my forthcoming adventure, little realizing what a horrendous experience the next four and one- half years were to be.

While at the recruiting office in Vancouver, I had met several other fellows going through the same process who eventually ended up with me on the same train for Brandon. They were Doug Gill from Chemainus, Harry Cooper from Powell River and Cliff Hazlett from Vancouver. We picked up Jack Ott and Howie Jones in Kamloops. The next morning in Revelstoke the two McKinnon brothers, Bill and Leo, Art

Switzer and another person boarded the train. We from British Columbia experienced our first prairie winter. It was about twenty below zero when we arrived in Brandon. A corporal with a truck and driver met us and transported the group to the depot.

The Manning Depot was housed in a large exhibition building right in the heart of the city. They had taken out cattle stalls, given the place a coat of whitewash, and installed a long row of sinks, showers and toilets to accommodate about four hundred people and filled it with double decked bunks. It was here that the rapid transformation from civilian to airman took place. We were given haircuts, issued with uniforms and advised of the do's and don'ts of this particular establishment. We were also given medical exams, inoculations, drill and physical training, plus lectures on wearing the uniform on and off base. Route marches through the streets of Brandon took place regularly every day regardless of weather. Our training went on for about six weeks and then we were posted to Dauphin, Manitoba.

When I say 'we,' I refer to our group of ten from B.C. who started out together and stayed together for almost nine months. We were to perform guard duties at the airfield south of Dauphin while it was under construction. We were given accommodation in partially constructed huts, issued a rifle and a clip of ammunition, and were assigned patrol areas to be guarded evening and night. This field was slated to be Number 10 Service Flying Training School, but at the present it was nothing but piles of frozen clay and stacks of lumber. Needless to say, our impression of guarding this place against sabotage caused us some hilarity. Our stay was longer than we anticipated but ended after two months. In this time the weather warmed up, and then we were constantly marching in gobs of prairie gumbo until our transfer to Number 2 Wireless School, Calgary, Alberta.

We arrived in Calgary and were placed in the 14th Entry at the school. The wireless course was quite vigorous, learning Morse code, radio theory, aircraft recognition, drill and physical training, for six days a week. Sending and receiving code was set at a speed of 9 words a minute. Shortly after, the speed was raised to 12, then to 16 and eventually to 19 words a minute. As I was having difficulty trying to reach 9 words, the constant raising of the speed left me and others very much behind. I attended extra evening classes in an effort to speed up but to no avail. Some were in the same boat as I, but most of the class succeeded in reaching this goal. An instructor advised those of us who hadn't it was not uncommon for people to fail, as their hearing or reception cannot adjust to the code at any speed. Others in the class passed the Morse code but failed the radio theory. However, we were six very disappointed fellows who had to await their future in the air force. Wireless Air Gunner was the last flying position available when I joined up. In the meantime a new flying category of air gunner was developed to man the extra gunner positions on the new four-engine bombers now coming into service. We had all enlisted to fly, but we thought our dreams were dashed until the new positions were announced and we could volunteer to re-muster to this new category. Five of us jumped at the opportunity and one elected to stay on ground duties. In retrospect, perhaps he was the smart one.

I found the air force life in Calgary to be very good. Discipline was strict, but they also treated us fairly. The majority of the fellows on course were great people. Doug Gill was a marvellous piano player and would entertain the guys in the evenings at the canteen. One night I got into the beer too much and found myself in my pyjamas in the shower at one o'clock in the morning. Gazing at this spectacle was the Corporal from the physical training section; he was the Duty Non-Commissioned Officer (DNCO) that night. Each of the staff N.C.O.s was required to do duty patrolling the school, barracks, perimeters and guard-room for security reasons. He quietly took me to my bunk. That is the last I heard of the incident until twenty years later when we met again. On this occasion he was an Inspector in the Calgary City Police and I was an Inspector in the

R.C.M.Police in Alberta. We had some great laughs over this incident.

During our stay in Calgary, we were issued with khaki summer uniforms. On the 24th of May, 1941, the entire 400 students of the school marched downtown in beautiful sunshine and warm temperatures for Queen Victoria May Day ceremonies. After the program we marched back to the school, and at this time the weather took a turn. It became extremely cold, windy and then snowed. By the time we reached the gates we were marching in three inches of snow, very cold, and everyone was soaking wet. The next morning we were back to blue uniforms!

We five who had failed the course and now wanted to re-muster as air gunners were sent to Trenton, Ontario. This whole procedure took about six weeks. During this time we met a group of New Zealanders who were going through the same process as we. Friendship was spontaneous. We were together for many months while at Trenton and during our training as air gunners. The New Zealanders had two native Maori with them, and the entire group put on a Maori war dance for the station, which was well received.

The New Zealanders were included in our group when I was transferred to Number 7 Bombing and Gunnery School at Paulson, seven miles east of Dauphin, Manitoba. Here we went through the exercises of taking machine guns apart and assembling them blind-folded, aircraft recognition and air-firing flying in old Fairy Battles, along with skeet shooting and rifle practice on the range. Upon completion we were presented with our air gunner's wing and promoted to sergeant. We were one happy bunch, as we would be flying, our greatest desire. We were given thirty days' overseas leave prior to departing for the 'Y' Depot at Halifax, Nova Scotia. Before we left Paulson we received some sad news. Our friend Doug Gill who had graduated as a wireless air gunner at Calgary, had been killed in a plane crash in eastern Canada. Apparently the Lockheed Electra he was flying in crashed into a hillside during bad weather. There were no survivors. The end of the course also brought about the separation of those who had been together for many months and the probability that we would never meet again. We were also getting closer to the theatre of war.

My embarkation leave at home went quietly. Brother Jim had joined the air force as a mechanic and was stationed at Patricia Bay near Victoria. He came home on leave and then I went back to Patricia Bay with him for a few days. We would not meet until several years later in England. He claims he tried to get into air crew but was rejected because of colour blindness. I used to accuse him of trying to gain the good side of father by being a mechanic. This statement, of course, would raise lively discussion. I still think I was right. I know my father was proud as punch of Jim, as he certainly let me know, while I was home. Family and friends came to the station to see me off. The Calverts presented me with a gift box containing cake, cookies, etc., and Margaret gave me a large wooden bowl of Yardley shaving cream. I carried that bowl of shaving cream for thousands of miles and all over England. The date was November, 1941, but I did not shave until 1944.

After five days on the train I arrived at Halifax, Nova Scotia, where we were transported to the 'Y' Depot, the assembly point for all Air Force personnel going overseas. I was here for about two weeks before boarding a ship. The base was a fair distance from Halifax and transportation difficult, so our trips were not too frequent. We had mainly to wait and think.

Two weeks later we were trucked to the docks, where we boarded an old converted luxury liner, the SS California. When I say 'converted,' that is exactly what they did; they took luxury out and put utility in. The crew was entirely Royal Navy; no civilian Merchant Marine types anywhere. Wooden benches had replaced all lounge furniture, the lounge windows were boarded up, and the portholes were painted over. The dining-room was stripped of its furniture and long tables and benches served instead. The smaller lounges were the sleeping areas. The bunks were stacked three high, allowing no room to turn over; you either slept on your back or your stomach. The toilets, or 'heads' as the navy called them, were entirely open air. Four decks above the water they had removed some of the railings and constructed toilets out over the side of the ship. There was nothing between your backside and the ocean, which was going by at about 10 knots, four decks below.

The Royal Navy tried to make this ship an armed merchant cruiser, equipped with four three-inch guns, magnetic anti-mine cable running around the entire ship and an acoustic device trailing behind to attract acoustic torpedoes away from the ship. I am very glad we did not meet any German pocket battleship like the *Bismarck* roaming about the Atlantic at this time; it would have made mincemeat of us. Our convoy consisted of ourselves, a minesweeper recently built by the U.S. for the Royal Navy, and a Polish destroyer that had escaped from Poland just prior to that country's being occupied by the Germans. The weather was absolutely rotten, which made the journey for the three ships a terrible ordeal. The captain advised us that this trip was one of the roughest he had ever experienced. While in the middle of the Atlantic, a radio message with black edges was posted on the notice board on the mess deck stating that Pearl Harbour had been bombed by the Japanese and a state of war now existed between the U.S.A. and Japan as well as Germany and Italy. This was indeed a black day for all.

We anchored in the Clyde opposite Greenoch close to Glasgow. The next day we disembarked onto tenders and were taken to the docks where we boarded a train for an unknown destination. That was December, 1941. Travelling all day and into the night, we arrived at Bournemouth on the English Channel.

Aircrew Pay in the

ROYAL CANADIAN AIR FORCE

The following are the scales of pay for R.C.A.F. aircrew at various stages in their training:

AC2. (upon enlistment) .... $1.30 per day.

LAC. Airman Pilot, Air Observer, or Wireless Operator (Air Gunner) (Received soon after training is commenced)... $1.50 per day.

If you are selected for training as pilot or air observer, after completing training at an Initial Training School, you will be entitled to a special allowance of 75 cents per day, in addition to pay and allowances to which you are entitled at the time selected. This special allowance is paid continuously for the whole period during which you are undergoing flying training.

Over and above the daily rates of pay you receive, in addition, your meals and living quarters. You are also clothed, completely at the government's expense.

When you are mustered as sergeants at the conclusion of your training under the British Commonwealth Air Training Plan, your daily rates of pay, including flying pay, are as follows:

Airman Pilots $3.70
Air Observers $3.70
Wireless Operators (Air Gunners) $3.20
Air Gunners $2.95

In addition to the above rates you are also still provided with meals, quarters and complete clothing.

Upon embarking for overseas with, or in conjunction with the Royal Air Force, your pay will be in accordance with the scale of pay and allowances of the Royal Air Force. The deficiency, if any, in this rate from that of the Royal Canadian Air Force will be issued to you by the government of Canada as deferred pay, either on termination of service or otherwise in special circumstances.

For those selected as officers, the daily rates of pay, including flying pay are as follows:

Pilot Officer $6.25
Flying Officer $7.00
Flight Lieutenant $8.50
Squadron Leader $9.75

Officers are allowed $150.00 towards the purchase of their uniforms.

R.C.A.F. RECRUITING CENTRES
ACROSS CANADA

VANCOUVER, B.C.	Merchants Exchange Building, Vancouver, B.C.
CALGARY, Alta.	1208-1st Street East, Calgary, Alta.
EDMONTON, Alta.	Provincial Building, Edmonton, Alta.
SASKATOON, Sask.	Birks Bldg., 153 Third Ave. S., Saskatoon.
REGINA, Sask.	New Regina Trading Co. Bldg., Regina, Sask.
WINNIPEG, Man.	Lindsay Bldg., 228 Notre Dame Ave., Winnipeg.
NORTH BAY, Ont.	40 Worthington Street East, North Bay, Ont.
WINDSOR, Ont.	Canada Bldg., 374 Ouelette Ave., Windsor.
LONDON, Ont.	Old Post Office Building, London, Ont.
HAMILTON, Ont.	275 James Street South, Hamilton, Ont.
TORONTO, Ont.	200 Bay Street, Toronto, Ont.
OTTAWA, Ont.	130 Queen Street, Ottawa, Ont.
MONTREAL, Que.	Post Office Bldg., 1254 Bishop Street, Montreal.
QUEBEC, P.Q.	53 Buade Street, Quebec, P.Q.
MONCTON, N.B.	Dominion Public Building, Moncton, N.B.
HALIFAX, N.S.	Broadcasting House, 10 Tobin St., Halifax.
CHARLOTTETOWN, P.E.I.	25 Kent Street, Charlottetown, P.E.I.

2. 1940 R.C.A.F. Recruiting Poster

3. Jack and Jim Routledge with dog Rinty at Mission, B.C. about 1930.

4. Author at home from Calgary Wireless School Easter 1941

5. Jack with his mother and brother Jim while
   on embarkation leave. Jim was home from
   Victoria for the week-end 1941.

6. Royal New Zealand Air Force members staging a Maori War Dance
   for an audience in Trenton, Ontario, 1941. (R.C.A.F. photo)

7. Graduation from Number 7 Bombing and Gunnery School,
Paulson , Manitoba, 8th November 1941. Back row (Left to Right)
Bruce Neal (RNZAF),Mel Cato (RNZAF), Jack Ott (RCAF),
T.L.Crear (RNZAF), M.Frizzel (RNZAF), G.Wunsch (RNZAF),
Front Row (Left to Right); Jack Routledge (RCAF), Pete
McKenzie (RNZAF), W.L.Redfern (RCAF), G.McDowell
(RNZAF). This is the same group of New Zealanders that
performed the Maori War Dance at Trenton. (RCAF photo)

This city is an historical community famous as a resort, but now these amenities were out of bounds to all except the local inhabitants and service personnel.

We were billeted in the many hotels until our postings came through for further training. Behind the city are the chalk cliffs, which have made the south coast of England famous. The cliff tops were honeycombed with trenches and bunkers. There was a promenade along the sea front and beautiful beaches with a long pier extending out into the Channel.

These beaches were now closed. Land mines had been buried there by the thousands, and on top of them were miles and miles of rolled barbed wire hundreds of feet wide. Large metal projections were buried in the sand to obstruct landing craft and other vessels. The beautiful pier had been destroyed to prohibit its use in case of invasion. The promenade was closed to all after dark and patrolled by armed sentries. Failure to respond immediately when challenged by a sentry could result in being shot. This description basically fits all the communities along the English Channel during this crisis.

In fact Great Britain was in a desperate situation. Since September, 1939, the Germans had invaded and occupied Poland, Czechoslovakia, Austria, Greece, Albania, Denmark, Norway, Belgium, Holland and half of France. The Germans had Italy and now Japan as its allies. The evacuation of British and French troops at Dunkirk had taken place, the Battle of Britain was fought and won, and the possibility of an invasion of Britain by Germany was very real. The battles in North Africa were not going well at all. Then the Japanese entered the conflict and things were going from bad to worse. To sum it up, Britain had its back to the wall but was determined to remain the only beacon of hope in Europe. This country was striking back with all its resources and hitting the Germans constantly. In a few short months I would become part of the force that was striking back.

Our daily routine at Bournemouth was the roll call parade at 8 a.m., followed by lectures on the security measures in the coastal region. Route marches through the streets were very frequent. The local citizens seemed to enjoy watching us; it probably gave their morale a boost just seeing all these service men marching by. Spitfires and Hurricanes would patrol the beaches regularly on alert for enemy aircraft hit and run raids. Shortly after we left Bournemouth, the Germans did pull a hit and run raid on this city, killing and injuring many civilians and airmen.

After several weeks we were moved from Bournemouth to Hastings, farther east on the coast, close to Dover. Here our routine was exactly the same while we waited for transfer to our flying training stations. Our accommodation was in a large, fairly new, beachfront hotel. We shared four to a room; the view was excellent from the fourth floor. The front of the hotel was on the promenade near the water which was totally out of bounds to anyone; access was by the rear entrance only. We watched the fighter patrols by day and the gun flashes across the Channel by night. We found many interesting things to do. We rode the double decked open top busses out into the country and back. The view from the top of the chalk cliffs was spectacular. Hastings had a pub in a cave, in which patrons like us took a great deal of interest. We attended movies, carnival shows, and wandered through the street like tourists, though the army strictly enforced security on the beachfront. After three weeks here, we were now on our move to further training at Number 7 Air Gunnery School at Stormy Down, adjacent to Porthcawl, South Wales.

Our new airfield was perched on a knoll overlooking Porthcawl on the Bristol Channel, about half-way between Cardiff and Swansea. One evening from our barracks we witnessed an air raid on Swansea, located to the west of us. Here I had an experience that almost caused me to use a parachute. We were flying in an old twin-engine Whitley III and upon returning from an air firing exercise over the

Channel, we found our base closed in with fog. Our pilot announced to the instructor and we four gunners that he would attempt to find an opening in the fog but, failing that, we were to put on our parachutes in preparation for bailing out. I thought this situation only happened in movies and of course we became very apprehensive. After we had circled the base for about half an hour, an opening appeared in the fog, the pilot dove through it and plunked the old aircraft dead centre on the runway. We were a jubilant group and I will never forget this pilot's flying skills.

We completed this course and on the 18th of March, 1942, I was sent to Kinloss in the north of Scotland and then moved to the satellite station at Forres. This was Number 19 Operational Training Unit (O.T.U.), which would be my last training unit before going on to an operational squadron. An O.T.U. was where all crews trained for actual wartime situations. An operational squadron was a squadron that flew combat, which was our ultimate destination. Here we were to fly in the old Whitley IVs, which were equipped with two Rolls Royce engines and carried a crew of five.

The forming of a crew was a very simple procedure. All flying trades gathered in the flight section, where the Commanding Officer advised all pilots that they would now go about selecting their flying buddies. I was sitting with a group of other air crew when a big Canadian asked me if I would fly as his gunner. I agreed. He chose the other three in the same manner. The Canadian pilot was Jack McDonald (Mac) from Victoria, B.C.; navigator, Harry Rowan from London, England; bomb aimer, Bill Wright from Saskatoon, Saskatchewan; wireless operator, Jack Gibbs from Bowmanville, Ontario. This selection process was completed in about an hour with no fuss or official interference. The five of us formed the nucleus of our crew and with the exception of Harry Rowan would be destined to fly together for the next three and a half years.

All crew members attended classes in their respective trades, and a few days later we had our first flight together.

We completed many cross-country trips, including bombing exercises, circuits, and landings mostly at night. These exercises were not without some problems. On one cross-country we had an engine catch fire. Fortunately, we were within a short distance of base and landed safely where the fire was extinguished. On another trip we had an engine failure which prompted a forced landing at Prestwick, Scotland, where we remained for two days until a mechanic and parts were flown in. The third incident occurred during a bombing exercise over a large island of solid rock near the Orkney Islands off the north coast of Scotland. When we released the bomb, a photoflash, shaped like a bomb, was released simultaneously. Its fuse would set it off at the same instant the aircraft camera exposed the film. The photo would be studied later to determine how accurate we were. The flash was extremely powerful, generating roughly a million candle power. This flare was carried in a metal chute inside the aircraft. When released, it would fall with the practice bombs and its safety pin would be pulled automatically by a wire lanyard attached to the chute. On this trip to the range, in very severe turbulence, the photoflash flipped out of the chute onto the floor of the aircraft causing the safety to be pulled and activating the timing device. It was directly behind Jack Gibbs's position, who immediately grabbed the device and rammed it back into the chute, where it exploded just below the aircraft a few seconds later. A piece of jagged casing came up the chute and lodged in Jack's right forearm, resulting in our returning to base immediately for medical treatment. Had the flash exploded in the aircraft, it would have destroyed the plane and us. In summary, other than having an engine fire, an engine failure, a near-catastrophic explosion and an injured crew member, we managed to graduate from this training establishment and proceeded to an operational squadron. We would now be actively fighting in the war.

Chapter 3

49 Squadron (R.A.F.)

1942 to 1943

On the fifth of June, 1942, we arrived at 49 Squadron, Scampton, located five miles north of Lincoln, a walled city with a Roman history, and a large cathedral with two spires overlooking the city. These spires could be seen for miles and would serve as our daylight landmark when flying, as our base was due north. Our timing was not the best; the squadron had just converted from twin-engine Hampdens to twin-engine Manchesters. Unfortunately the engines in the Manchester had proven to be a total failure caused by malfunction resulting in heavy losses. Yet we continued using these aircraft for training while awaiting the arrival of the Lancasters. During this quiet period some Manchesters were sent on a bombing raid and two failed to return. The following day, 5 Group launched a dinghy search for the crews off the German Frisian Islands in the North Sea. Two Manchesters from 49 Squadron were detailed and I was selected as rear gunner to fly with pilot Sgt. Cumberland, Royal Australian Air Force. We returned 6½ hours later; however, the second search aircraft failed to return. We were advised that this search constituted an operational trip as we were very close to the German Frisian Islands. To indicate a daylight operational trip we wrote the entry in our log books in green ink. These log books were then submitted regularly to the Squadron Commander for certification. Upon reviewing the squadron records after the war, I note this particular flight is not rated as an operational trip. As far as I am concerned, however, I will still claim it as my first.

On the 22nd of July, 1942, the new Lancasters arrived of which one was assigned to our crew. It bore the serial number R5751 with 49 Squadron identity AE-E. We were very proud of our new charge. Our crew spent many hours converting to this four-engine aircraft and becoming familiar with its capabilities. We practised take-off and landings, two and three engine overshoots, day and night cross-country navigation, practice bombing, air firing exercises and fighter affiliation. This last exercise replicated coming under attack while in flight. A Spitfire from a nearby fighter squadron came to our station to act as the enemy. We would then fly over the North Sea, with the fighter chasing us and the gunners giving evasive action calls to our pilot. It was great sport, but the gunners and the pilot were kept hopping. When the exercise was completed, we would waggle our wings and the Spitfire would close up alongside us and follow us home.

As I mentioned earlier, the Germans occupied only the northern half of France. Our first operational trip as a crew was a leaflet raid over Vichy, France, on 11th of August, 1942. This was really a training exercise of flying over enemy territory, dropping the leaflets, taking a picture of the city and returning. I have been asked what was on the leaflets. I had no idea as it was all in French, but I would presume they were to boost the French morale. Continuing our operational flights, on August 15/16 we laid sea mines near the Frisian Islands: 9 aircraft- missing. On 27/28 August we conducted a raid on Kassel: 306 aircraft-31 missing, 10.1 percent of the force. We bombed Nuremburg on the night of August 28/29: 158 aircraft-23 missing, 14.5 percent of the force.

Our bombing raids were carried out at an altitude of 12,000–18,000 feet and with a few exceptions, always at night. This type of operation was therefore very hazardous because of enemy fighters, flak, risk of collision and the severe and unpredictable European weather, particularly in the winter months. The losses for these trips were quite high and were attributed to conducting bombing raids in the full moon periods. At times the moon was so bright I swear I could have read a newspaper in the rear turret. This situation also worked in favour of the German night fighters. Moreover, we at times would leave vapour trails which the fighters followed like a map right to our exact positions.

Flak is anti-aircraft fire, light or heavy. 'Light' means from a machine gun, approximately 20 mm with an effective range of 10-12,000 feet and the shells explode on contact. 'Heavy' flak refers to predicted flak from (88 mm) heavy anti-aircraft guns. The altitude, direction, wind and speed of the aircraft is predicted on ground radar from which the guns are calibrated to these predictions and the shell has its fuse set to explode at the prescribed altitude. This type of heavy flack became extremely accurate as the 88mm had the capability of firing rapidly to over 40,000 feet.

On September 6/7, 1942, we bombed Duisburg: 207 aircraft—8 missing, 3.9 percent of the force. On 8/9 of September we attacked Frankfurt: 249 aircraft—7 missing, 2.8 percent of the force. September 10/11 we bombed Dusseldorf: 479 aircraft—33 missing 7.1 percent of the force. On September 13/14 we attacked Bremen: 446 aircraft—21 missing, 4.7 percent of the force. On September 14/15 we bombed Wilhelmshaven: 202 aircraft—2 missing. On September 16/17 bombed Essen: 369 aircraft—39 missing, 10.6 percent of the Force. September 18/19 laid sea mines in the Gulf of Danzig in the Baltic near Poland: 5 aircraft lost. 23/24 September, bombed Wismar: 83 aircraft—4 missing. 24/25 September laid sea mines in the Baltic: 1 aircraft lost. Some of these flights were very long, over the North Sea, Denmark, to the Baltic and return, keeping us airborne for over seven to nine hours.

Our home station at 49 Squadron was in a state of fluctuation. The twin-engine Hampdens had been taken out of service and replaced by twin-engine Manchesters. They in turn had been found to be a failure. Then to create more confusion, extra personnel were arriving to bring each crew number up to seven. The Squadron had surplus navigators, wireless operators and flight engineers, all looking for an opportunity to join a crew. As a result Jack Gibbs was put back as a mid-upper gunner and we acquired a wireless operator who flew with us for the next eight trips. Finally we received Sgt. Higginbottom as flight engineer to complete our crew of seven.

Harry Rowan, our navigator, suffered from chronic airsickness, which became a concern to all of us. He managed to get through the Operational Training Unit (O.T.U.) at Forres and we completed eight operational trips, but on the ninth he caused pandemonium. While en route to the target of Dusseldorf we ran into heavy turbulence and Harry became extremely ill. Upon arrival at the target we were coned by searchlights and subjected to heavy flak; we were forced to take violent evasive action which meant the nose down and violent turns right or left to avoid the lights and shells. We were fortunate, but we dropped from 12,000 to 6,000 feet over the target, where we became fair game for light flak. Our navigator by this time was violently sick, all his instruments and charts had been thrown to the floor. He was on his hands and knees searching for his material when his oxygen became disconnected and he began to lose consciousness. We completed our bombing run and Mac turned the aircraft in the general direction of home. Harry was so ill he was helpless. Bill Wright, Jack Gibbs and Higginbottom managed to recover the necessary material, and between them and the pilot we arrived back safely but very concerned. The next day Mac had a long conversation with Harry and advised him that he was going to have him grounded immediately for medical reasons. This came about. A year later we heard Harry was in India as an air traffic control officer. He was a good navigator who did not want to quit.

We acquired a spare navigator every time we flew - Tom Bennett, John Allin and others, until eventually we obtained Geoff Bellamy on a permanent basis; he remained with us for over two years. Tom Bennett ended with Jerry Fawke's crew, and Allin flew one trip to Bremen in September, 1942, which was successful, and each crew member was issued with a certificate from 5 Group Headquarters. This document certified that we had successfully bombed the aiming point. Then Sgt. Higginbottom was also removed from the crew because of deafness at high altitude. I could hear over the intercom the pilot shouting instructions to the poor guy, but he was completely oblivious to what was going on. A medical board ruled him unfit for any further flying duties. Sgt. Partington (R.A.F.) took over this position but again was taken off after several trips because of airsickness. Sgt. Ken Stauffer (R.C.A.F.) from Ontario replaced Partington and remained with us to the end of our 49 Squadron flying. During all this upheaval Jack Gibbs was returned to the wireless operator's position and we acquired Sgt. Gordon Blair (R.C.A.F.) of Winnipeg as our mid-upper gunner. He also remained until the end of this tour. Every crew member in his own way suffered from anxiety which was quietly overcome without burdening the other members of the crew or affecting your duties. However, when you have a member who is not able to function because of medical reasons, the tension heightens and places all in peril.

John Allin stayed on the squadron and flew with another crew. Many years later in 1998, his son Dr. John Allin of Grantham, Lincolnshire, wrote me inquiring if I could recall his father's flying with us in 1942. He said that his father had been killed on the 13th of February, 1943, while returning from a bombing raid on the German submarine base at Lorient, France. Apparently his aircraft struck balloon cables outside Plymouth harbour and all were killed. The Royal Navy sent down divers to retrieve any bodies, but none were found in or near the aircraft. What happened to the crew remains a mystery. Did the aircraft suffer damage from enemy fire and all bailed out and the aircraft flew on by itself, eventually hitting the balloon cables? This theory seems likely, as all crews were briefed to stay away from heavily defended English coastal targets, such as, Plymouth, when on their return trips. To this end, all balloons were equipped with radio transmitter squealers that had a radius of about ten to twelve miles and sounded in all crew members earphones. These squeals were a warning that we were too close. The Allin aircraft was well below normal altitude when it struck the balloon cables. The possibility also exists that they were unsure of their position and thought they were over land.

Taking to a parachute over a large expanse of water would not have been the approach we would have taken unless the aircraft was on fire or out of control and about to crash into the sea immediately. There was always the alternative of ditching the plane in the ocean, taking to the dinghy and chance being located by R.A.F. or German search and rescue. The odds of survival were far greater in a dinghy than floating about in a life jacket in either the North Sea or the English Channel. We were all advised that the survival time in these frigid waters was approximately six minutes unless you managed to get into a dinghy and even then the possibility of perishing was very real. The Allin aircraft apparently was not in dire condition, as it flew on and into the balloon cables. Whatever prompted seven men to abandon the plane will never be known. Ironically this attack against Lorient, France, would be the last trip on our first tour.

Dropping sea mines in the German shipping channels was carried out by Bomber Command and code-named 'gardening.' (See Appendix B.) The Royal Navy would identify the main shipping routes on the German North Sea and the Baltic to indicate where we would sow our mines. We would carry on average four to six mines depending on the distance from England. The mines must be placed precisely in order to gain maximum effect. They had to be dropped from an altitude of 150 to 300 feet above the water. As soon as the mine was released, the parachute would open, and upon entering the water it would sink to the bottom; salt water would immediately activate the parachute release mechanism, the lower portion of the mine would remain on the ocean floor as an anchor, and the salt water would dissolve the parachute material. The explosive portion would then float up tethered to a cable to a pre-determined depth and await a ship to pass over or near it. These mines were activated by acoustics or magnetically. Aircraft laying mines did so on dark nights at low altitudes, the risk of hitting the water or a ship always present. On one occasion, enroute to laying mines at Peleau in the Gulf of Danzig, we flew low level over the North Sea across Denmark where we nearly struck an old, three-masted schooner anchored in a bay on the Baltic side. A German flak ship opened fire on us, but we managed to get away unscathed. When we reached our target area at Peleau, and made our run to drop the mines, we became engaged in a running gun battle with anti-aircraft guns on the shore. Fortunately, we sustained no damage, as we had a long trip home - 9 hours and forty-five minutes total flying time.

Sea mines were frequently laid in the Baltic and North Seas because of extensive use of these waters by German coastal shipping. After Germany occupied Poland and later declared war on Russia, they shipped thousands of tons of supplies destined for the German front from North Sea ports of Belgium, Holland and Germany through the Kiel Canal into the Baltic Sea. Here the supplies were off-loaded near the German battlefront in Lithuania, Estonia, Latvia or Russia. These shipping lanes became a great concern to Russia, who requested Churchill to do what he could to curtail their use. Intelligence reports advised that our sea mining operations had sunk many ships and had caused the Germans to employ more ships and personnel to clear the channels.

Mining was an extremely hazardous duty. Usually, one aircraft was dispatched at night to a specific area and carried the mines each measuring about eight feet in length, two feet in diameter and weighing approximately eight hundred to a thousand pounds. Depending on distance and the fuel load, the aircraft would carry four and some times five to six. To avoid radar detection the pilot flew at a maximum altitude of 500 feet or less. This tactic required great skill and concentration as well as accurate navigation, since it would be very dark and in many instances the weather over the North and Baltic seas would be poor. There was always the risk of running into a ship or passing close to a flak ship and the ensuing gun fight could bring about disastrous results. Then there was the possibility the pilot would lose concentration on his flying and hit the water surface at over 200 miles per hour. Once we were in the general area for the drop and close to landfall, we would attempt to establish an accurate position, then make our timed run from that point. We would drop our mines from an altitude of not more than 300 feet, keeping speed at normal cruising and flying straight and level. Each mine is released separately at timed intervals. When all were dropped, we set course for the long trip home. We could never relax, as we were aware the enemy knew of our presence and would have flak positions alerted and night fighters searching for us.

October, 1942, was a quiet month, mainly because of bad weather. On October 1/2 we bombed Wismar in northeast Germany: 78 aircraft—2 missing We landed at Acklington because of bad weather at our home base of Scampton. On October 13/14 we bombed the heavily defended naval base at Kiel: 288 aircraft—8 missing, 2.8 percent of the force. On October 15/16 we attacked Cologne: 289 aircraft—18 missing, 6.2 percent of the force. October 17th we made a daylight raid on the Le Creusot armament works in the French Alps: 94 aircraft—1 missing. On 23/24 of October we bombed Genoa, Italy: 122 aircraft—3 missing. On the 24th of October we conducted a daylight raid on Milan, Italy: 88 aircraft—3 missing.

All our attacks had been at night, but when they ordered us to practise formation flying, which we did on several occasions, we suspected something else was planned for us. Le Creusot was a very large French armaments factory in the French Alps where the Germans controlled production which was for the German forces. On the 17th of October, we learned why we were practising formation flying. We were briefed to attack the factory in daylight to ensure accuracy and avoid French casualties. As we would be flying well beyond the range of fighter escort, the route to the target was plotted from England southwest over the Atlantic at a very low altitude, then turned east to come in over the Bay of Biscay. We had to remain low to avoid radar detection, but approaching the target we would climb to ten thousand feet for our bombing run. The British Broadcasting Corporation announced to the French, one half-hour before our arrival, that the factory was going to be bombed. Our bombing was accurate, the factory and powerhouse were heavily damaged and French casualties were very low. Since we bombed just before dark, we were able to fly north across France and back to England in darkness, thus avoiding enemy fighters. 94 Lancasters took part in the raid, and only one was lost over the target. Both the front and mid-upper turrets suffered damage on a Lancaster when birds struck them while was flying low over France to the target. Another aircraft had engine trouble over the Bay of Biscay and was returning to his base when he was attacked by three German Aredo floatplanes. In the ensuing air battle the Lancaster gunners shot down two of the floatplanes and the third took off badly damaged. The flight engineer on the Lancaster was killed and others wounded, but they managed to get back to England.

The Egyptian campaign at this time was going well for the British Forces. The Italian Army in the desert was wiped out and hundreds of thousands taken prisoner. This war was not popular with the Italian population, and with very little prompting they would turn against Mussolini. We were therefore directed to attack the Italian cities of Genoa, Milan and Turin. Our route to these cities was straight south across occupied France, over the Alps and return; average flying time, 8 to 9 hours. We attacked Genoa again on November 7/8: 175 aircraft—6 missing, 3 percent of the force. On November 29/30 we attacked Turin: 228 aircraft—3 missing. The total number of operational trips for November was low because of severe weather conditions over Europe.

On one Italian trip while over France, our high-pressure oil reservoir blew up, filling the entire front of the aircraft with a fine mist of hydraulic oil. Everything and every person, except me, in the rear turret, were soaked in oil. We now had no operating gun turrets, flaps or under-carriage. The Lancaster had emergency air tanks to operate the flaps and under-carriage, but using them on landing was a one shot deal. Once they were down, there was no way to raise them in case of an over-shoot. However, Jack McDonald put the aircraft on the runway just as though everything were fully operational. On another trip back from Italy, we lost an engine, so it was shut down and the propeller feathered and we flew home as though nothing were wrong.

When in an operational bomber squadron, all flying crews were given seven days' leave every six weeks because of the tremendous stress that they endured. Bill Wright had an aunt, Jane Wright, living in Leigh, Lancashire. I was always invited to her place with Bill every time we had leave and she treated us like royalty. We would relax, go walking all over the town, visit an Uncle Frank who was a coal miner and join him in the pub for a few pints and a game of dominoes. Our leaves were short and sweet.

On December 6th, 1942, we were in our favourite aircraft, R5751, returning from more practice formation flying. Just as Jack touched down on the grass runway, the starboard tire blew, and the wheel hub dropped into the turf, where it dug in; we then went down the runway at about 100 mph doing large ground loops and ploughing up the turf at the same time. Damage to the aircraft was severe; the starboard outer engine was damaged and part of the wing were ripped off and the fuselage was twisted, but we walked away. Had the runway been cement, there probably would have been a fire, and an entirely different outcome.

The Lancaster was repaired and we were requested to give it a test flight, which we did. In our view the aircraft was unfit for operational flying because of many faults, one of which was flying with the right wing low that no amount of trimming would correct. We were given a new Lancaster and we picked it up at the factory. Old R5751 was put into training. I noticed that after the war it ended up at a Conversion Unit and survived.

On off-duty times, we would journey into Lincoln to visit the pubs, eat fish and chips and socialize with fellows from other squadrons around Lincoln. Our preferred pubs were the Saracen's Head, the Bull, and the Black Swan, and they were always packed. The crowding became markedly worse when the Americans arrived to build their airfields.

Most squadrons had a spare aircraft and a spare crew. The spare aircraft was to replace any Lancaster that was in for maintenance or to replace one that became unserviceable prior to take off in order to maintain the squadron strength. The Lanacaster would be held available with a full bomb load and fuel. The spare crew would fly other aircraft while the assigned crew was on leave. The captain of one these crews was Flying Officer Tony Eyre, R.A.F. Friendly relations between his crew and ours led to trips to the pub together and other recreational activities. On one occasion when we went on leave, Tony was assigned to our aircraft. Upon our return he mentioned quite casually that our aircraft had suffered a minor mishap the night before. Going out to the dispersal to check, we found the starboard wing tip had a gaping hole. Fortunately, the fuel tanks were untouched as was the main wing spar. Tony explained that the large hole had been caused when a bomb dropped from another aircraft while it was flying above him over the target. Lucky for Tony and his crew the bomb did not explode. We gave Tony a bad time about the poor way he looked after other people's property. This friendly bantering went on for some time. The aircraft was repaired that day and we were back in the air.

Jerry Fawke's crew consisted of Navigator Tom Bennett from England, Bomb Aimer Earl Osler from Regina, Saskachewan, and Wireless Operator Paul Fortin from Flin Flon, Manitoba. We also associated with this crew quite regularly and became close acquaintances. Earl was a bit of a handsome fellow with a Clark Gable moustache. While on a trip over Germany, Earl was on his hands and knees over the bomb sight and had just dropped their bombs when a light anti-aircraft shell exploded in their bomb bay, blowing open the inspection hatch right behind his backside. The exploding shell filled his posterior with chunks of hot steel, but fortunately no others were injured. This wound became a great subject of discussion and jokes for some time afterwards.

Earl Osler remained in the air force and is now retired. He and Tom Bennett came to visit me in 1993 when Tom was here visiting from England after retirement from his accounting business. They said their pilot Jerry Fawke was then living in London, England.

Our flying exploits did not go unnoticed. Jack McDonald was awarded the Distinguished Flying Cross which was presented to him by King George VI at an investiture in Buckingham Palace. The crew went to London, and although we were not allowed in the palace for the ceremony, we certainly celebrated afterwards. In our eyes Jack was a worthy recipient of this award.

Jack's investiture in London gave us the opportunity to act on an on-going problem—our promotions. When serving in an R.A.F squadron we were under the direct command of the Royal Air Force, which meant we would serve on their stations. Our Royal Canadian Air Force Headquarters (R.C.A.F.) in London, however, acted as though they did not know we existed. The line of promotion was as follows: A person enlisting in the R.C.A.F as air crew was given the lowest rank, Aircraftsman 2nd class (AC2), and six months later he was promoted to Leading Aircraftman (LAC). Upon graduating from his flying training, he was presented with his wings and promoted to sergeant, or in some instances given the commissioned rank of Pilot Officer. One year later the sergeant was promoted to flight sergeant, then warrant officer. All of our crew with the exception of Mac, the pilot, held the non-commissioned officer (N.C.O.) rank. We would meet other Canadian air crew in Lincoln and find that they had their promotions despite the fact they were quite junior in service to us.

We took the opportunity to visit R.C.A.F. Headquarters in London as we firmly believed they were embarrassed by the oversight. They wanted a picture of our crew, they arranged an interview on the B.B.C. which broadcast to Canada and, of course, they promised to examine our records. Shortly after this visit all the Canadians in our crew received their promotions and back pay. Several weeks later both Bill Wright and Geoff Bellamy were awarded the Distinguished Flying Medal. R.C.A.F. Headquarters had no responsibility in making these awards. The squadron makes the recommendations for decorations.

Meanwhile a new air base was constructed at Fiskerton southeast of Lincoln which was to serve as our home for the remainder of our time with 49 Squadron. The two squadrons at Scampton were moved out to make room for the formation of 617 Squadron commanded by Guy Gibson, later to be known as the Dam Busters. Fiskerton was anything but ready, only partially finished with mud everywhere. Mess halls were not completed nor were the barracks. Moving aircraft on the station was hazardous. If a wheel ran off the cement taxi strip or runway, the whole wheel disappeared in the mud and the plane might suffer structural damage, particularly if it was loaded with fuel and bombs.

During December, 1942, we were again blessed with very bad weather which certainly curtailed our activities. We were able to complete only two trips. December 8/9 to Turin, Italy: 133 aircraft—1 missing. On December 9/10 as we were over France en route to Turin, the main hydraulic reservoir blew out causing us to make an immediate return to base, 227 aircraft—2 missing. On December 20/21 we bombed Duisburg, Germany: 232 aircraft—12 missing, 5.2 percent of the force. Our crew had now completed 24 trips of the thirty required for a full tour.

On January 16/17, 1943, we bombed Berlin: 201 aircraft—1 missing. Berlin was bombed again on January 17/18: 170 aircraft— 22 missing, 11.8 percent of the force.

These trips were to let Hitler know that Berlin was just as vulnerable as London during the Blitz. He and Goering had boasted that no British bombs would ever fall on Berlin. These raids were Churchill's response. On January 27/28 Dusseldorf was bombed: 162 aircraft—6 missing, 3.7 percent of the force. January 30/31 Hamburg was attacked: 148 aircraft—5 missing, 3.4 percent of the force.

In February 1943 we completed two more trips and brought our flying career with 49 Squadron to a close. One trip was to Whilhelmshaven U-boat yards on February 11/12: 177 aircraft—3 missing. The other was to Lorient submarine pens on the Atlantic coast of France on February 13/14: 466 aircraft—7 missing, 1.5 percent of the force. Both targets were heavily defended but our bombing was very accurate.

All five of our crew had finished their first tour; Flight engineer Ken Stauffer and mid-upper gunner Gordon Blair had to remain and finish their required thirty trips. We five had mixed feelings about this accomplishment. The policy at that time was that every air crew member who completed a tour of operations must take a leave of absence and spend it on a training unit as instructor in his particular field. As for Canadians, all air crew were sent back to Canada for thirty days' leave after which they must return for a second tour. The irony of this policy was that it split up good and experienced crews with little possibility of their ever getting together for the second round. We had some pretty serious meetings to reach a decision. As a consequence we four Canadians decided against coming home but elected to request transfers for all five to the same training unit. This was approved to the delight of all of us, especially our English navigator. We were then assigned to our respective duties at Number 29 Operational Training Unit at North Luffenham. My work as a gunnery instructor took place at the satellite station of Woolfox Lodge about ten miles distant.

Next page –

8.   Bomber Command and its Targets

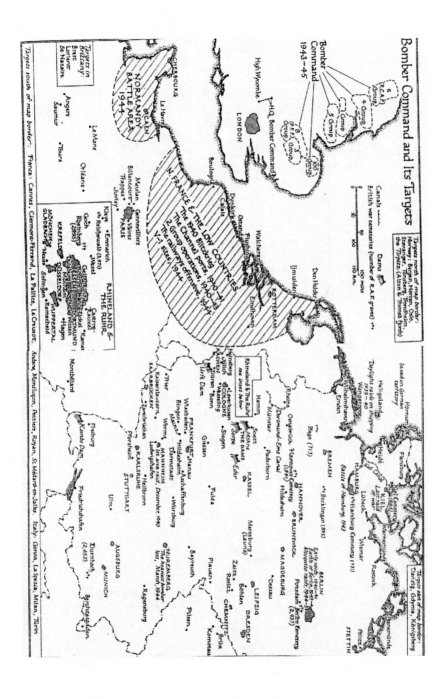

9. Crew photo taken at R.C.A.F. Headquarters London, England, 1942, following McDonald's investiture at Buckingham Palace. A good reason to celebrate, which we did. (Front) Geoff Bellamy, Jack McDonald; Jack Gibbs; Bill Wright; (Back) Jack Routledge and Ken Stauffer. (R.C.A.F. photo)

10. 94 Lancasters flying across central France from the Bay of Biscay heading for the le Creusot munitions factory near the French Alps on the 17th of October, 1942; our aircraft is somewhere in this photo. (Air Ministry photo)

LANCASTER BOMBLOADS

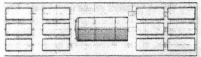

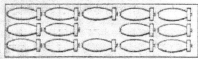

Blast and Maximum Incendiary Area Bombing Raids against general targets (most common load). One 4,000lb Amatol, Minol or Tritonal-filled, impact-fused High-Capacity (HC) bomb (Cookie), and 12 Small Bomb Containers (SBC) each loaded with 24 30lb or 236 4lb No.15 Incendiary or No.15x Explosive Incendiary bombs.

Industrial Demolition Area Bombing Raids against factories, railyards, dockyards. 14 1,000lb Medium Case (MC), General Purpose (GP) RDX or US short-finned High Explosive (HE) bombs. With mix of instantaneous (nose-armed) and long-delay (up to 144 hours, tail-armed) fusing.

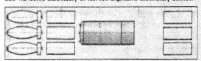

Blast, Demolition and Fire Area Bombing Raids against heavily industrialised cities. One 4,000lb impact-fused HC bomb, three 1,000lb short-finned, short-delay, tail-armed HE bombs, and up to six SBC's with 4lb or 30lb incendiary bombs.

Blast and Demolition Area Bombing Raids against heavy industrial areas. One 8,000lb Mk.I or III, HC bomb (two 4,000lb 'cookies' joined together) with barometric or impact fusing, and up to six 500lb MC or GP bombs with instantaneous or long-delay fusing.

Medium-Range Low-Level Attacks against general targets. 6 x 1,000lb bombs, tail-armed with mix of 11 sec to 60 min delay fusing. Capacity limited (in 1942) by use of long-finned bombs, up to 3 x 250lb GP bombs sometimes added.

Maximum Incendiary Area Bombing Raids against general targets. 14 SBCs, each loaded with 236 4lb No.15 and No.15X (1 in 10 mix) bombs.

Carpet Bombing of Tactical Targets such as V-1 sites, radar sites, armour concentrations. 1 x 4,000lb HC, impact-fused bomb and up to 18 x 500lb MC or GP bombs, short-finned with mixed instantaneous and delay fusing.

Raids On Docks, Fortifications, Ships, Etc. Up to six 2,000lb armour-piercing bombs with 0.05 sec delay, tail fusing. Three 500lb MC, SAP or GP, or 250lb GP bombs frequently added.

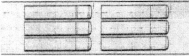

Air-Sea Minelaying Sorties against Docks, Ports, Seaways. Up to six 1,850lb parachute magnetic and/or acoustic mines.

Maritime Anti-Submarine Patrol. Six 500lb and three 250lb (Mk.I, II and III) anti-submarine bombs fused for sub-surface detonation, and five 250lb SAP bombs, tail-armed with 0-2 sec delay for surface attack (not used after 1942).

'TALLBOY' operations against Submarine Pens, Battleship Tirpitz. One 12,000lb deep penetration, spin-stabilised bomb containing approximately 5,760 lb of Torpex D.

'GRAND SLAM' operations against Submarine Pens, Viaducts, Underground Factories. One 22,000lb deep penetration, spin-stabilised bomb containing approximately 11,000lb of Torpex D.

11. Each rectangle indicates the size of a Lancaster bomb bay and the load configurations from bombs to sea mines are shown in each. The size of the load was dictated by the distance to the target; the longer the trip, more fuel and smaller bomb load.
(Art Work by David Howley)

12. Armourers manoeuvring a 4000 pound bomb into position for hoisting into the bomb bay of a Lancaster. This is only a partial load. Note the 500 pound bombs on the trolleys in the background. The three tags are the safety-pins in the fuses which are pulled automatically upon release. (Adrian Balch photo)

13. Flying low over the English Channel on our way to Milan, Italy, in daylight. Lancaster EA-E from 49 Squadron with Jack McDonald at the controls and the author in the rear turret. (Wing Commander Slee photo)

14. Another picture of McDonald Lancaster flying with 88 other other aircraft low over the English Channel to avoid detection from German radar while nearing the French Coast on 24th of October 1942. (Wing Commander Slee photo)

15. Photo taken over the Swiss Alps by Sgt. Jack Gibbs from the mid-upper turret. (Jack Gibbs photo)

16. Another Lancaster with us over the Alps on our way to Milan. The raid was carried out at dusk and we returned to England over France in the dark. (Jack Gibbs photo)

Chapter 4

Life in the Air and on the Ground

During my writing I have referred to 5 Group squadrons and others. I will now endeavour to clarify the basic structure of the Royal Air Force. The air force was formed into commands: Fighter Command, Bomber Command, Coastal Command, Training Command, etc. Each command was subdivided into groups. Take Bomber Command, for example, as it is the one I was most familiar with. Bomber Command was headed by Air Marshal Arthur Harris, and his command was broken into Groups numbering 1, 2, 3, and so on. Each group was under the command of an Air Vice Marshal and had a set number of bomber squadrons with 18 to 20 bombers on each. The majority of the stations had two squadrons. The station commander was a Group Captain and each squadron was commanded by a Wing Commander. The squadrons were then broken into Flights A and B with the flight commander for each having the rank of Squadron Leader. A few exceptions to this pattern existed, particularly with specialized squadrons, such as, Pathfinders.

I served with Bomber Command in 5 Group on 49 Squadron in A Flight at Scampton, Lincolnshire. The station at Scampton was shared with 83 Squadron. Our station was commanded by Group Captain Whitworth and our squadron by Wing Commander Slee. The 'A' Flight Commander was Squadron Leader Barnard. I do not recall the 'B' Flight Commander's name. The command system was simple, comprehensible, and worked well.

Previous chapters outline our operational trips to bombing targets in Germany, Italy and in some instances, France. The mine laying or 'gardening' has also been explained. But I have not attempted to explain the extreme tension bomber crews experienced at all times whether flying on operational missions or not. Germany had occupied all of Europe except England, Switzerland, Spain, Portugal,

Finland and Sweden. Bomber crews flying out of England had many miles of hostile territory to fly over in order to reach their targets in Germany or Italy and return by the same route. The Germans had established numerous fighter bases in these occupied territories along with a sophisticated radar system and had set up anti-aircraft batteries at all major cities or targets of any significance. They were determined to prevent us from bombing the Fatherland, but the defences could not stop us from overwhelming them and we penetrated deep into Germany. Italy was given the same treatment to let Mussolini know they were not untouchable. However, none of these objectives was accomplished without Bomber Command paying a very heavy price.

The Americans became operational in 1943 and elected to bomb during daylight hours. As a result German targets were being bombed day and night. This type of offence caused the German High Command to place great emphasis on defence by building more fighter aircraft and anti-aircraft guns and deploying thousands of troops from the Italian and Russian fronts to man these armaments. It is stated that Germany was forced to employ in excess of a complete division, approximately one hundred thousand people, to man their defences, plus Hitler was denied the use of his top line aircraft, heavy artillery (88 mm) and precious fuel in the Russian theatre where they were desperately needed.

In contrast to the Americans, Royal Air Force bomber crews flew the majority of their trips at night and so were denied the luxury of having fighter escort on most trips. Only a few sorties were flown in daylight. There were no trips where the crews sat back and relaxed. We were in a state of nervous tension every day from the time we learned of a pending raid that night, at the briefing for the raid, during preparation, at take-off, over enemy territory and upon return. Not until we were back on terra firma could we begin to relax. All days were the same, even on training flights over England, which went on constantly. We had to be on constant alert for our own aircraft, or for German intruder aircraft over England hunting for us.

The normal daily routine was to report to the Flight Section at 10 a.m. for roll call. At this time we were advised of the results of the previous night's raid and our losses and advised whether another was planned for the coming night or what training exercises we were to undertake. When operations were announced, all squadron personnel went into high gear: from cooks, armourers, fuel truck drivers, electronics personnel, mechanics, to the photo section to name a few. Information that came in on the teleprinter from Group H.Q. was decoded by the Intelligence Section and prepared for the briefing of air crews. At the same time, fuel capacities and bomb loads were sent to the fuel and armament sections. The air crews would go each to their respective dispersal point, inspect their aircraft with the ground crews and, if necessary, take it for a local flight to check out any problems.

Several hours before take-off, the crews would report for briefing, where they would be advised of the target, the route to and from, weather, intelligence report on defences, take-off times, total number of aircraft on the raid, and so on. During this time the ground crews were pumping thousands of gallons of fuel into the aircraft and armourers were hoisting bombs into the bomb bays. The fuel and bomb loads varied with each raid, and depended on the distance. A large bomb load and less fuel indicated a short trip, possibly the Ruhr Valley, a trip of four or five hours' duration. Anything over five to ten hours meant less bomb load and more fuel. An extra hour of fuel was always provided as a safety measure to allow for landing at another base because of weather, or navigational error. Our maximum fuel capacity was two thousand gallons, which gave us a range of 2500 miles with a 7000 pound bomb load.

Weather in Europe was always changing, creating a constant alert to flying conditions whether local flying or on operations. The meteorological section of Bomber

Command, referred to as the 'Met. Section,' worked hard to bring forward a weather report that turned out right. A weather report at the briefing would give the crews their prediction of what to expect on take-off, going to, over the target, on our route home, and what to expect at our base. Just prior to a raid taking off, the Met. Section would dispatch a Spitfire and in later years a Mosquito to check their predictions over the target route and report back. While we were on our way to the target, our wireless operator was receiving, in code, reports on the changes to the wind speed and direction at our altitude, which he passed on to the navigator and pilot. Clear weather over the target was always critical, but in later years with the use of radar (H2S) we were able to bomb through thick cloud. Upon return we always had the threat of smog, ground fog or low hanging rain clouds that might obscure the hills and other obstructions on an approach to landing. When landing was not possible, the crews were diverted to other stations that were clear.

Our people did their utmost to get the weather predictions right. On some occasions they were right on and other times they were very wrong. Predictions would be for thin layered cloud over the North Sea to Germany, but in some incidents we would run right into large electrical storms that caused us some concern. When airborne the wireless operator would let out a trailing aerial that extended about 150 to 200 feet behind the aircraft. In these storms I could see the trailing antenna illuminated its entire length with a blue glow as were the muzzles of my machine guns, and the front end crew said the propellers were also lit up. We would be loaded with fuel, bombs and electricity, not a very healthy cargo.

England was and is still an industrial country. With the war production required, all the factories were spewing out smoke and other pollutants in great quantities. Adding to this situation was the fact that central heating for a home in those days was a luxury. Practically every residence had a fireplace in each room of the house and when used, each of these fireplaces would add to the already heavy pollution lying over the land from five hundred to a thousand feet. There were days we would be out on practice flights and fly over the pollution where visibility was restricted. We referred to this bluish-grey smog as industrial haze through which it was possible to look straight down and see ground detail, but when coming into land, this haze made horizontal visibility limited.

During the winter months, take-off time was between 5 p.m. and 7 p.m. In the late spring, summer and early fall we would depart at 9 p.m. or 10 p.m. Suppers would be served to air crew immediately after briefing; then we would go to the Flight Section and put on our flying gear. Busses transported the crews to the dispersal points where the aircraft were parked. Before changing into our flying clothes, every crew member was required to search his pockets and remove any letters, bus tickets or other item that would disclose the whereabouts of his station to the enemy should he be shot down. The only documents that we were allowed to carry were our escape kits. These consisted of detailed silk maps of the countries we would fly over on this particular trip, plus currency for each country, and were stored in waterproof pouches. The buttons on our battle dress were designed so the top could be screwed off and a compass revealed. Each crew member was issued with a small folder with the basic language of each country translated into English. Many of us carried a small pocket Bible. Each crew member was issued a revolver, but I did not carry mine. When a person takes to his parachute over enemy territory, his chances of being caught were extremely high, and carrying a revolver could precipitate a shoot-out with some trigger-happy soldier or farmer. The emphasis was to avoid capture but, if you were caught, give the enemy only your name, rank and serial number. At the same time always be alert to chances of escape.

There was no aircraft heating in the rear or mid-upper turrets of a Lancaster. My flying gear consisted of long silk underwear over which I would put my uniform shirt and a heavy white turtle-neck sweater, then my battledress jacket and trousers. Over this again was an electrical suit that looked similar to coveralls but had electrical elements sewn throughout. Electrical gloves and slippers snapped to terminals on each arm and leg of the suit. On top I then put on leather, fur lined trousers, jacket, boots and leather gloves followed by a Mae West flotation jacket and a parachute harness. Then the scarf and helmet. The helmet was equipped with an oxygen mask, microphone and earphones. The microphone was fitted with an electrical heating element to prevent my breath from freezing on it at high altitudes. The electrical elements plugged into the aircraft's electrical supply in the turret. The mid-upper gunner was dressed the same, as temperatures in the winter while flying at 18.000 feet were usually minus 40 to 45 degrees Celsius. Finally, to improve the rear gunner's vision, the Plexiglas (plastic enclosure) was removed and he was left totally exposed to the elements. Needless to say when all this gear was worn, we were not ready to run a marathon. The pilot, navigator, engineer, bomb aimer and wireless operator were in the heated forward section and required only a fur jacket over their uniform and fur-lined boots.

Pilots were the only persons aboard these aircraft who used the seat-type parachute; all other crew members wore the chest packs, which had to be stored in a rack near the crew member's position. The rear gunner's chute was stored in a rack just inside the aircraft. When required, he would rotate the turret to face the rear, open the doors behind him, lean back inside the aircraft, retrieve the chute from the rack and hook it to the harness on his chest. He then had to make a choice of exit. He could rotate the turret to the side, open the doors and fall out backwards into space, hoping his feet did not become tangled in the turret controls, guns and other equipment and leave him dangling by his legs out the rear of the aircraft. Or, while the turret was still facing to the rear, he could get out of the enclosure, crawl up a small catwalk in the fuselage, over the stabiliser and rudder spar, and the chemical toilet, and jump out the main side door. This escape route sounds so simple; however, as the situation would be compounded by the emergency, the aircraft could be on fire, in a spin, or upside down, and any personal movement was extremely limited. Rotating the turret, should there be a hydraulic failure, was accomplished with a small hand crank on the lower right side.

Each air crew member was issued with his own parachute and harness. This permitted the recipient to adjust and fit his harness to his personal comfort, depending on how much extra flying gear he was required to put on first. The climate in England is quite damp, so a rotation of parachutes was required. Every three months the Parachute Section would call in your parachute and give you a spare. Your chute was opened, strung up in a loft to air dry for several days, at which time you exchanged the spare for your regular parachute all folded and packed. The girls in this section had quite a sense of humour; on giving you back your regular parachute they would comment, "If this one doesn't work, bring it back and we will replace it."

Upon arrival at the aircraft by bus or truck, each member of our crew would relieve himself on the tail wheel as a gesture of good luck. We would be in the air for a long period, access to the chemical toilet was not recommended, particularly using the portable oxygen supply at high altitudes over enemy territory. Upon boarding the aircraft each member placed his chute in a rack, took his position and checked out all the equipment. The pilot and engineer would do the cockpit check, start the engines, warm them up, then check with each crew member for readiness. When the appropriate time arrived we would taxi for take-off. The planes would be lined up nose to tail on the taxi strip waiting their turn onto the runway. As soon as the aircraft ahead of us started his take-off, we would taxi onto the runway and wait for the green light signal from the controller who was in a small trailer at the end of the runway. Radio silence was absolute as the Germans would be monitoring our frequencies for any sign of activity. This silence remained until our return to England.

A Lancaster's empty weight was 30,000 pounds (15 1/2 tons) but fully loaded with fuel and bombs it would weigh near 60,000 pounds (30 tons). The first few minutes on take-off were critical and intense. At the end of the runway, the pilot would lock the brakes, set the flaps, do a quick instrument check with the engineer, and upon receiving the green light from the controller from his little trailer at the end of the runway, the pilot would wind up the engines to maximum throttle and then release the brakes. We would charge down the runway with four Rolls Royce engines delivering 1640 horsepower each, and the engineer calling out the air speed to the pilot. Once the wheels were off the ground, the pilot would call for 'wheels up.' At this juncture disaster could strike. All that was needed was for one engine to lose power or fail completely and the fully loaded aircraft would hit the ground. The results of such a crash were disastrous to crew and aircraft but unfortunately they did happen. Once airborne with wheels and flaps up and at flying speed, the engines would be throttled back and then we started the climb to our assigned cruising altitude. Further checks were done and the navigation lights turned off. My job was to remind the skipper about the lights, as we had seen bombers over Germany with them on, not a very healthy thing to do.

After take-off and for the remainder of the trip, all crew members except the navigator and wireless operator were on constant alert to avoid collisions with our own aircraft and to scan for the enemy. Collisions did happen all too frequently and in these situations rarely were there survivors. Weather permitting, the bomb aimer would attempt to sight the enemy coast and give the navigator some help in pinpointing our position, as the electronic aids he used were subject to jamming by the Germans. The navigator would give the pilot the course to steer and be working on the next one on his table behind black-out curtains. The wireless operator would constantly monitor frequencies, receive any messages from Group Headquarters, decode them and report to the pilot and navigator. The engineer would monitor all engine gauges, fuel tanks and calculate our consumption. We two gunners constantly scanned the blackness around us watching for our fellow aircraft and the enemy. We maintained absolute silence on the intercom except when we had something to report. Useless prattle as shown in American movies between crew members about girl friends and other unrelated matters was taboo. Long periods of time would pass when there was nothing to report. Mac would call us every ten minutes and check on our well-being. Over the target, intercom discipline was essential, as the navigator and bomb aimer would be giving instruction to the pilot.

The possibility of collision over the target was very real, as 100 to 800 bombers concentrated over an area for a period of twenty to thirty minutes. Into this melee anti-aircraft fire exploded around us and searchlights probed the sky for a target to assist their night fighters. Bomb explosions on the ground plus ground fires which lit up the sky were a great help to us but also to the night fighters. We had several very near collisions with other aircraft. On one occasion, while on our way to a target another Lancaster passed roughly fifty feet overhead. The mid-upper gunner sounded the alarm, but by this time it was too late to take evasive action. I looked straight up from my turret into the darkness to see this huge black silhouette of a Lancaster with his exhausts glowing in the dark. It was so close I felt I could have reached out and touched him. Our pilot kept the aircraft on course as the other slowly slid from the starboard side to the port side and disappeared into the night, his engine noise drowning out our own. Now, that was close! We felt quite sure that the other crew did not see us at all. For a few long seconds there was no conversation. I guess we were thinking how damned lucky we were.

Immediately after dropping our bombs, we would alter course and head for home. This was not the time to relax, but some crews did and with near fatal results. By now the German Air Force knew we were in the area, their radar searching out our return route in an effort to bring about night fighters in large numbers. We would observe tracer bullets in the night indicating a fighter attack on someone. Upon reaching roughly fifty miles from the coast, we would put the nose down to gain extra speed without damaging the engines and clear enemy territory quickly as possible, dropping down to 8 – 10,000 feet. When crossing the English coast, we had to be constantly on the alert for our own coastal convoys, heavily defended cities and balloon barrages. It was not uncommon to be shot at by the gunners on the little coastal convoys running up and down the English coast. Upon nearing our base we would spot a beacon flashing particular code letters which signified it was ours. We could then fly a set course from the beacon to bring us over our base, and at this point radio silence was broken to obtain landing instructions. The runway lights would be turned on and advice would be given as to our landing number and altitude to circle, as there would be fifteen to eighteen aircraft all seeking permission to land. A priority was given to crews with injuries or aircraft damage. No matter how tired you were, staying alert was paramount to avoid collisions and watch for German intruders who would endeavour to blast you out of the sky while on landing approach. If intruders were detected, the control tower would advise "Bandits, bandits," and we would extinguish all lights and continue our circuit or return to the beacon and circle at a prescribed height until the all-clear was given. After landing and taxiing to our dispersal point, we would be greeted by our ground crew who would be advised of damage or mechanical problems. We then proceeded by bus to the Base H.Q. where each crew was interrogated by an intelligence officer. Supplied with a tot of rum by the padre, we would go along to the mess for bacon and egg. By this time it was 4 or 5 a.m., but sleep did not come easily, as you would be thinking about the previous activities and the fear that you might miss roll call by 10 a.m. at which time the same routine would begin again.

Each hut was usually shared by fourteen men of two crews, and so it was a matter of great concern the next morning when waking to find the beds of the other crew empty. It could mean one of two situations: they had been shot down, or they had landed at another station because of damage or mechanical problems. We usually got the sad news when we reported to the Flight Section for roll call. The C.O. would advise of over-all losses plus those of our own squadron, if any. The British Broadcasting Corporation would also broadcast every morning after a raid that the Royal Air Force Bomber Command had carried out bombing attacks on a certain target and 10, 20, 30 or more of our aircraft were missing. Each and every time we heard these statistics we would multiply the losses by seven crew members to determine our casualties. Some so-called documentaries have said that bomber crews were never informed of their losses as it would have a severe effect on their morale. This statement is absolutely untrue. We were kept informed and knew exactly what was transpiring at any given time.

Our seven crew members had now been together long enough to learn from each other. We not only flew together, we also shared our ground time as a crew also. To put our relationship in perspective, we were a team at work and at play. This attitude did not evolve from a plan, it just grew with time. In the air we became a very disciplined and close-knit group, we respected each person's ability to do his job well, and this belief in turn gave each one the confidence that was needed. I am not saying this approach was wholly responsible for our surviving thirty trips. A large measure of this equation was sheer good luck. When the chips were down and we were in a desperate situation, each of us knew the others could be relied on. There was no panic, no emotion, just calm and cool exchange of conversation as required.

Flight Lieutenant John Robert McDonald, known as 'Mac', was captain of the aircraft and superior to every person on board regardless of rank. Every one in the crew had a nickname and Mac was no exception. We also referred to him as 'the old man,' as he was the oldest at twenty-three years of age. Mac was from Victoria B. C., the son of a blacksmith. He was at least six feet two inches tall with a very muscular build and had been with the Canadian Olympic Rowing Team in Australia prior to the war. He had a happy-go-lucky attitude, which could be deceptive, as he was very intelligent, an excellent pilot and demanded the best from his crew. He stood solidly behind his crew-members if and when required. I often like to relate the story of Mac in the early stages of our time on 49 Squadron. Upon our arrival we four were the only Canadians on the squadron for approximately three months. Mac was the only Canadian and officer in our crew in the Officer's Mess. One Royal Air Force Engineering Officer made it quite clear he had no time for the people from the "Dominions" or the "Colonies." One evening when Mac was having a few drinks, this officer started expounding on Canadians. The lounge and bar of the mess was on ground level with very large swing-out windows and on this particular evening they were open. The Englishman kept on harping so Mac grabbed him by the scruff of the neck and seat of the pants and threw him right out the window onto the lawn. No damage was done except to his ego. The following morning Mac told us what had happened and warned that this scuffle might precipitate our transfer. He and his victim were summoned to appear before Wing Commander Slee, the squadron C.O., who admonished them both for their behaviour, and that ended the matter.

Geoffrey G. Bellamy, our English navigator, was a delightful person to work with. His home was in Ledbury, Hertfordshire, where his mother and sister lived and where Geoff spent his leaves. He was extremely intelligent and had numerous talents, particularly in the arts. When in the pubs, he would take a one pound English bank note from his pocket, prop it up and proceed to sketch it in detail on a piece of paper. We used to joke about his becoming a counterfeiter. Nothing rattled him. He was always cool and calm under stress and able at the same time to carry on with whatever he was doing. While on our operations Geoff was always very clear and concise, and some of the exchange between him and Mac would cause us all to chuckle. Geoff would give Mac a course to steer; for example, 150 degrees. Mac would repeat and alter course. It would be quiet for some time when Geoff would say, "Mac, I said 150 degrees, not 153." After a moment of silence, we could feel the aircraft altering course. Mac would apologize to Geoff and add they must get these compasses checked as there was a discrepancy between them. On the ground Geoff would tell all of us that he had checked the compasses earlier and there were no variances. Mac was just allowing the aircraft to wander a bit.

William Ruben Wright was our bomb aimer from Saskatoon, Saskatchewan. Bill's duties changed rapidly after we came to the squadron. His initial training was on a bomb-sight, but later with the introduction of H2S radar, he had to learn the whole new procedure of bombing while sighting on radar. As the radar screen was located on the end of the navigator's table and was also used to assist in navigation, both these men were under the black-out curtain.

John C. Gibbs was from Bowmanville, Ontario, and a very quiet person who gave the impression of being a deep thinker. He was good at his work as wireless operator. He would always participate in any activities that went on and had a wonderful sense of humour. He had a brother in the army stationed in England who would spend his leaves with us. He was not allowed to fly in our aircraft, although there was some thought of smuggling him aboard.

As stated previously, we were finally assigned a full-time flight engineer named Ken Stauffer who was from southern Ontario. This fellow had a big smile, a sense of humour to match, and knew his duties extremely well. He and the mid-upper gunner Gordon Blair had to remain and finish off their first tour. I know they both accomplished this goal and returned to Canada.

Our ground crew – the fitter, riggers, armourers, radio and radar technician – all played a major part in our success. They took extreme pride in their aircraft, working long, hard hours in all weather, night and day, to keep these machines fully serviceable. It did not matter what time we took off, they were there to assist in starting, and on our return in the wee small hours of the morning, they were again on the job greeting us and genuinely happy to see us back. These people were the unsung heroes of every bomber squadron and, it goes without saying, very little recognition has ever been given for the extremely difficult task they carried out. In my view, they greatly assisted in the successful conclusion of this war.

While at North Luffenham Operation Training Unit (OTU) following my first thirty operations, I was posted to the satellite station called Woolfox Lodge. This was a beautiful place, a vacant estate house on a slight rise at the edge of a small lake, and the airfield was built on flat land below with the usual cluster of buildings and huts. My function was to take four gunners at a time into the air in Wellingtons and shoot at a sleeve-target, called a drogue, being towed by another plane. The towing aircraft was also a Wellington equipped with a winch and nine hundred feet of cable. Later I spent time flying in the tow plane with Sgt. Jimmy James, R.A.F. As the aircraft was equipped with dual controls, I got a lot of practice time flying back and forth on the range, which was over the Wash near Norfolk. I became quite proficient and Jimmy allowed me to perform landings, which I accomplished with a great deal of nervousness and sweaty palms.

For his part Jack McDonald was sent to training base to practise beam approach blind landings in twin-engine Avro Ansons. In these cases the student was under a hood and the instructor alongside passing on instructions. Landing rights were signalled with red or green Aldis lamps from a person in a small trailer at the end of the runway. The instructor would relay the colour of the lights to the student who would then proceed to make an instrument landing. Somehow the fellow at the end of the runway became confused and gave two aircraft the green signal at the same time. Jack proceeded to carry out his landing procedure as instructed. At about 200 feet off the ground there was a loud bang as Jack's Anson came down on top of another that was underneath, and the two locked together and crashed onto the end of the runway. Jack ended up as the only casualty, when one of the propellers from the other aircraft came through the floor of his aircraft and sliced a piece off his heel. This accident caused our crew a great deal of anxiety because his injury might have grounded him and adversely affected our plans for a second tour together as a crew. However, Jack McDonald was a big healthy fellow and after hobbling around for a while he healed fully.

While at Woolfox Lodge I had my first experience with a person suffering from malaria. Sergeant Bob Lewis, R.A.F and gunnery instructor, had just returned to England after completing a tour of bombing operations in the Middle East. We were in the flight section when I noticed him turning yellow, and then he developed the shakes. I loaded him into a small van and took him to the medical building. He was back with us in a few days and confided that this illness is recurrent for the rest of his life. He had survived a tour of operations, but mother nature had blessed him with a bug that would haunt him forever.

The Short Aircraft Corporation constructed a four-engine bomber called the Sterling and although it was used on operations for a while it was never very successful. One day as a Sterling flew over our base with fire and smoke streaming from the starboard outer engine, the pilot made a quick turn and approached our runway. He touched down quite hard, and when it came to a stop, the fire truck responded, and the crew evacuated the aircraft. The Sterling was from a training unit and had seven air gunners on board plus an instructor and pilot. All appeared unscathed considering the hair-raising experience they had just been through.

Our entire unit was moved to Bruntingthorpe and the satellite station, Bitteswell and North Luffenham, was turned over to the Americans. We carried on as usual. I applied for a Gunnery Leader's Course and was accepted. This course was held at Number 1, Air Armaments School at Manby,

Yorkshire. Should I have wished to obtain a commission in the Air Force as a gunner, I had to successfully complete this course, and I did so in six weeks.

Upon my return the crew held another pub conference and discussed our going back for a second tour. It was a unanimous decision, as all of us had had enough instructing experience, and we volunteered to go back for round two of operations. Mac said he had heard that 405 Squadron (R.C.A.F.) had just joined the newly formed Pathfinder Group and suggested he fly to Gransden Lodge and meet with the Commanding Officer, Group Captain Johnny Fauquier. We all agreed, and several days later Mac advised that we were accepted, as they were only taking experienced crews, and we should hear from Number 8 Group Headquarters, Pathfinder Force, in due course

Chapter 5

405 Squadron (R.C.A.F.) Pathfinder Force

1943 to 1944

Our posting to the new squadron came in roughly two weeks, but first we were sent to Navigational Training Unit at Upwood. Here all crew had to learn the fundamentals of navigation, astral reading of the stars, map reading and all matters related to the subject. We looked a strange bunch, walking along country roads on clear nights while Geoff, our navigator, pointed out the various stars and their significance, interrupted only by mumbling and grumbling when one of the crew fell into a ditch in the black-out. As a rear gunner, I was always able to see where we had been, but never where we were going. This map reading course from my point of view was a bit of a farce as we always flew at night. So, in order to read a map, I would have to turn it upside down and switch on my turret light. For the benefit of the instructors, I went along with this process well knowing it would never be required.

While at Upwood, we acquired flight engineer Wilbur Wright R.A.F. from Birmingham and mi-upper gunner T.D. (Tommy) Duff from Winnipeg. Both these fellows had completed their first tour with other squadrons and we were very happy to have them.

Prior to the formation of Pathfinders, bombing was a hit or miss situation. Whoever arrived over the target first would drop his bombs on what he felt was the aiming point, and all others followed in behind him. This system led to inaccuracy and disappointing results. Pathfinders were in 8 Group, consisting of eight squadrons of heavy bombers and one squadron of Mosquitoes. The function of Pathfinders was to carry certain types of flares and ground markers, and with accurate navigation place these in the aiming point. The main force of 300 to 900 bombers would follow and bomb the markers. It was established that many bombers arrived late over the target, so some Pathfinder units were also placed late in the stream to reset the markers for these stragglers. A master of ceremonies was also added and improved results. His function was to be first on the target, drop his markers, then climb above and circle while giving instructions by radio to other bombers to correct their drop if it appeared the raid was wandering off the mark. This job was extremely dangerous, as the master of ceremonies would be over the target first and remain for at least one-half hour and sometimes longer, fair game for any of the defences.

Our arrival at 405 Squadron (Pathfinders) was a sad one. The squadron had been out on a raid that night and upon their return found all bases socked in with fog. Planes were diverted to other bases but the same problem existed. The situation became desperate as they were now low in fuel so crews were advised to point their aircraft towards the North Sea, set the automatic pilot and bail out. Some obeyed the order, others did not and chose to attempt a landing. The majority succeeded in coming in, but others were not so fortunate and they crashed killing all on board. 405 Squadron lost two aircraft on this occasion.

Group Captain Johnny Fauquier, a Canadian, Commanding Officer of 405 Squadron, was a tough and demanding individual, and he had to be. When Pathfinders were being formed, the Royal Air Force did not include any squadrons from the Commonwealth even though Canada was sustaining an entire bombing group of about ten squadrons in Yorkshire, plus thousands of air crew and tradesmen scattered throughout the world in the Royal Air Force. The Canadian Government insisted that a Canadian squadron be included in Pathfinders, as Canada was by far the largest contributor to the air force compared to any other country, excluding England. The Royal Air Force reluctantly agreed and 405 Squadron was selected.

Under these circumstances Fauquier insisted on the best performance from his crews to demonstrate that we were as good as or even better than others. He demanded perfection from every crew member and all ground staff. When there were no operational trips planned for a night, we would be flying practice navigation, bombing exercises and air firing. Fauquier flew on most operational trips with his crew, and upon return all crews were debriefed and Fauquier would personally analyze each crew's performance and advise the skipper if he thought it was not up to expectations.

The other crew that shared our hut had an Australian skipper. One night we were heading for Berlin, and all aircraft came out of their dispersal points in sequential order onto the taxi strip and proceeded nose to tail to the end of the designated runway. Upon our return we learned that the Australian from our hut ran off the edge of the taxi strip and when the wheel hit the soft turf, the aircraft sank to its hub and brought the whole take-off procedure for those lined up behind him to an abrupt halt. Since these aircraft had to be turned by tractor, the take-off was delayed by at least a half an hour. The Australian reported that his air compressor had malfunctioned causing brake failure, and he had run off the taxi way to avoid hitting the craft in front of him. Fauquier, this officer, and the engineering officer went to investigate this aircraft, started the motor that ran the compressor, and found that the air pressure came up immediately and remained constant. He apparently was over-using his brakes and had run his air supply down quicker than it was being generated.

When we returned that night from the flight, we found there were seven empty beds in our hut and all their personal belongings were gone. We thought this was strange until we found the reason the next day. Fauquier had ordered them off the base that night, and believe me, they left. We never did hear of this crew again. This C.O. was tough but everybody respected him and made the performance of this squadron the envy of others. Fauquier eventually took over from Guy Gibson V.C., the C.O. of the Dam Buster Squadron, and thus became the first Canadian to Command an R.A.F. squadron. Fauquier's replacement was Group Captain Reg. Lane, one of our squadron's flight commanders.

One day Jack McDonald went into Cambridge and purchased a car. It was a large Austin with all the trimmings including a bar in the back seat. He said it belonged to a movie actress before the war and she had sold it because of the shortage of gasoline. Mac had a lot of fun with this car, and then, to the surprise of all, Jack Gibbs bought a little Austin that was so small it was difficult to squeeze three men into it. The purchase of these cars led to some great times for our crew. We were able to travel to local pubs that were too far for our bicycles. When Mac or Gibby ran out of gasoline ration coupons, we would run the cars out to the aircraft dispersal and take the aircraft for a test flight. Amazingly when we returned to the car, the fuel gauge would read full. Our ground crew were absolutely incredible when it came to maintenance of the aircraft and two cars.

One night we drove to a local dance at a village about ten miles away. As we were leaving after having a great time, Griffith, a member of another crew from our squadron, asked for a ride home. Mac agreed and told him to stand on the running board and hang on, as there was no room inside. On the way home we were all singing and upon arrival at base not a person noticed there was no Griffiths. We went to bed. The next morning while we were at the flight section, another squadron Lancaster taxied to the control tower and opened the door. Two crew members jumped out and assisted a third person hobbling on crutches down the ladder. The Lancaster then left. It was Griffiths. He was some hostile, as he said he could be lying on the side of the road dying but nobody in our car cared. He further informed us that he was going to transfer to the squadron that had picked him up, given him medical care and brought him back. This he did. The squadron he transferred to was in 100 Group. They did all sorts of tricks with electronics and other means to confuse the Germans, plus ferried spies in and out of France and dropped arms to the underground. At the time the activities of this group were rated as very secret. I believe Griffiths survived the war. Where he came from in Canada I have no idea.

Another incident with the cars happened when we all travelled forty to fifty miles away to Welwyn Garden City for an evening at the pubs. Jack Gibbs had an old friend, Paul Fortin, a wireless operator, visiting from another squadron. Paul flew with Jerry Fawke's crew when we were at 49 Squadron. After an evening in the pubs a little spat broke out between Jack Gibbs and Mac, so Jack and Paul Fortin left in Jack's little Austin. About an hour later the rest of us departed for the base, and about half-way there we saw two very dim, shrouded headlights on our side of the road. It was Jack and Paul and they were going home backwards, as apparently the little car's gears had locked in reverse. We suggested that they park the car and pile in with us but, still miffed, the response was "No," and so we left them. These two arrived back at the base at 4:00 a.m. with very stiff necks. Next morning at the flight section we had a lot of laughs over the incident. Paul Fortin, who was from Flin Flon, Manitoba, survived the war and remained in the R.C.A.F.

We settled into normal operational squadron routine and became acquainted with new faces. We had some successful raids and made significant contributions to others. All our crew had now been commissioned as officers. I will certainly thank our skipper for his input, as he made the recommendations. We were close to our fortieth trip, we felt we had earned the promotions, and of course the usual celebrations were in order.

Flying from England over enemy territory was not a relaxing occupation, as tensions ran high at all times. The secret was to keep your anxieties under control, do the job and work with the other six as a team. We accomplished this harmony all the years we flew together, and I don't mind saying we were envied by other crews. This is not to say we did not have our differences at times as we had been together for a long period, but we were now like brothers.

While at Gransden Lodge a Royal Air Force pilot by the name of Reg Gardner was the beam approach instructor who took pilots up in a small Oxford aircraft and practised blind landings using a radio beam. Reg took a liking to our crew and would join us on our pub nights. One night after many drinks the crew got into an argument with Mac and told him that we wouldn't fly with him again. Mac countered by saying he did not care, as he was fed up with us. Reg Gardner was appalled at the turn of events and pleaded with everybody to make amends, but to no avail. The next morning at the regular roll call, we were all sitting and talking when Reg came in and presumed we were still upset with Mac. Mac played along and we followed suit, leading Reg almost to the point of break-down. We then advised him that the tiff we had had the night before was finished when we got home and this was another new day and a sober attitude. We were amazed at his genuine relief so all apologized for leading him on. Reg always wanted to get into operational flying, and shortly his opportunity came to fly Mosquitoes on Pathfinders when he was transferred to a squadron at Whyton near us. One night while taking off, his aircraft swung on the runway, careered across the field and crashed into the control tower killing his navigator and himself. Ironically, Mac was selected as a member of the board of enquiry into this tragic accident.

We started operational flying with 405 Squadron (Pathfinder) on December 20/21, 1943, with a trip to bomb Frankfurt: 650 aircraft – 41 missing, 6.3 percent of the force. On December 23/24, during the early hours of the morning we bombed Berlin: 379 aircraft – 16 missing, 4.2 percent of the force. On December 29/30 we attacked Berlin: 712 aircraft – 20 missing, 2.8 percent of the force. This flight was the commencement of what we referred to as the Berlin milk run. In January, 1944, we made six more trips to the German capital wishing Hitler a happy new year on January 1, 1944. Berlin: 431 aircraft – 28 missing, 6.7 percent of the force. We were attacked over Berlin by a FW190 fighter, which was shot down by gun fire from both gunners; there was no damage to our aircraft. Needless to say, this incident caused some anxiety. The encounter also indicated that by using single engine aircraft as night fighters, the German defences were becoming desperate. The fighters were part of a program the Germans called Wild Boar, which allowed these single engine aircraft to roam about unhindered by instructions from ground control. Bomber Command only allowed us to claim this FW190 as damaged.

On January 2/3 we bombed Berlin: 383 aircraft – 27 missing, 7.0 percent of the force. On January 5/6 we bombed Stettin: 348 aircraft — 16 missing, 4.5 percent of the force. On January 20/21 attacked Berlin: 769 aircraft – 35 missing, 4.6 percent of the force. January 21/22, Magdeburg: 648 aircraft – 57 missing, 15.6 percent of the force. Again on January 27/28 bombed Berlin: 515 aircraft — 33 missing, 6.4 percent of the force. Back to Berlin again on January 28/29: 677 aircraft – 46 missing, 6.8 percent of the force. On January 30/31, 1944 bombed Berlin: 534 aircraft – 33 missing, 6.2 percent of the force. Eight raids on Berlin during the latter part of December and all during January of 1944 took the toll of 279 aircraft, mainly four-engine bombers with a crew of seven. A quick calculation reveals that over 1900 persons were lost in what was referred to as the Battle of Berlin and it was by no means over. Each time we would not know of our destination until we were in the briefing room when the curtain was opened on the large wall map showing Berlin, and the crews, uptight, would groan, "Not again!"

Early February was a quiet time for us because of inclement weather that allowed the crews to have a much needed rest. On February 15/16 we were back to Berlin: 891 aircraft — 43 missing, 4.8 percent of the force. On February 25/26 we bombed Augsburg: 594 aircraft – 21 missing, 3.6 percent of the force.

On March 1st attack on Stuttgart: 557 aircraft – 4 missing, .07 percent of the force. Stuttgart was again attacked on March 15/16: 863 aircraft – 22 missing, 4.3 percent of the force. March 18/19 Bomber Command attacked Frankfurt: 846 aircraft – 22 missing 2.6 percent of the force. March 22/23, attack on Frankfurt: 816 aircraft – 33 missing, 4.0 percent of the force. Two years earlier Bomber Command had ceased carrying out night raids during the moon period as the moon greatly assisted the enemy night fighters. However, this policy was ignored for the next raid on Nuremburg because the Met. people had predicted high cloud en route with no cloud over the target. A Mosquito making a meteorological flight to the target prior to the raid had reported that the predicted protective cloud was not there. Despite this report the raid was not cancelled and we proceeded as usual, with tragic results for Bomber Command. The date was March 30th 1944; Bomber Command attacked Nuremburg: 795 aircraft – 95 missing, 11.9 percent of the force. Multiply the missing aircraft by seven and you will have a good indication how many members of Bomber Command were lost in this raid.

All the data, e.g. dates, target, number of participating aircraft, number of missing aircraft and percentages were obtained from the historical record book *Bomber Command War Diaries* by Martin Middlebrook and Chris Everett, published by Penguin Books, London, England. This book documents every raid carried out by the Royal Air Force Bomber Command from 1939 to 1945 and in some instances gives a short narration on the effects of the raid as obtained from German and Italian records. The data obtained coincided with the entries in my own log book and Squadron documents.

The bomber offensive against Germany was quickly gaining momentum. We were bombing by night and the Americans by day on targets supplying the German war machine. We attacked submarine pens, diesel engine factories, electronic plants, refineries, munitions plants, tank and heavy armament manufacturers; such as the Krupp Works. We also carried out raids against major cities, such as, Berlin, Hamburg and Nuremburg. These raids were not carried out without severe losses to Bomber Command, as the Germans were continually developing new countermeasures in the electronic field and developing new fighter aircraft and tactics.

Mac was promoted to Squadron Leader and became deputy flight commander. At the same time he was awarded the Distinguished Service Order. Flight Engineer Wilbur Wright, Navigator Geoff Bellamy, Bombardier Bill Wright, Wireless Operator Jack Gibbs, Mid-upper Gunner Tommy Duff, and Rear Gunner Jack Routledge were all awarded the Distinguished Flying Cross. This accolade came as a complete surprise to all of us though we secretly felt we deserved some recognition for our success and longevity. We were also cognisant of our requirement to complete a second tour. That goal appeared to recede as time went on, as our losses rose, along with our anxiety about outwitting fate. However, we did have the satisfaction of knowing we were a rare crew whose every member was a commissioned officer and who had all received decorations, some twice.

On the night of January 30th, 1944, while returning from Berlin, we were over central Germany at approximately 18,000 feet. The night was dark and the ground below absolutely black, not a light showing anywhere. Suddenly a series of flashes appeared directly below us. I reported to Mac the heavy anti-aircraft fire below. Mac immediately threw the aircraft to the port with nose down and full power. In the air space we had occupied, a series of 88 mm shells exploded exactly at our level but a little to starboard. A plastering of shrapnel spattered just forward of the rear turret and along the fuselage and on the wing. Plotting us on their radar, the Germans missed us by a mere few yards. Had the gun flashes on the ground gone unnoticed, and had we not taken evasive action, they would have made direct and fatal hits on us.

When we returned to base we went over the damage with the ground crew and marvelled at our luck that nobody was injured. Then we hopped aboard the bus that had been waiting at the dispersal point to take us to interrogation. Geoff Bellamy joked that he must have wet himself as the inside of his flying boot was soaking. When we were taking off our flying gear in the locker room, Geoff pulled off his boot to find it was full of blood and in the calf of his leg was a piece of shrapnel about the size of a twenty-five cent piece. The metal had come through the wall of the aircraft, through his boot and clothing, and lodged in his leg. He had not felt any pain. The hospital repaired him and he was flying the next day determined he was not going to miss any trips.

On our 47th trip, which was to Frankfurt, while returning from the target, we had another narrow escape. Again it was pitch black and I sensed there was something behind us, only lower down. I reported this possible sighting to the rest of the crew and Mac said he would maintain his speed and height and wait to be advised when identification had been established. I thought it was one of our own, as it stayed at our speed for a time, then suddenly closed in. I gave Mac directions to turn hard to starboard; at the same time I opened fire as I had identified the aircraft as a Junkers 88 night fighter. Both the mid-gunner and I saw our tracer shots hit the aircraft, but he returned no fire and disappeared into the dark. We were allowed to declare this encounter as an enemy aircraft damaged. We speculated on why he had not closed in immediately and opened fire before I saw him. We felt he was vectored to our area by ground radar and then used his own radar to get close enough to obtain a visual sighting of us. At this point the pilot takes over from his navigator and determines the angle of attack. We concluded that the navigator had got him to our general position, but the pilot could not yet pick us out visually, and it was at this point I saw him first. The luck did not always fall this way for bomber crews.

Air gunners were taught how to make sightings on very dark nights and on this occasion the system worked. When the gunner is constantly rotating his turret scanning the darkness and senses there is some object at a certain position in the dark, he does not stare directly at the object in an effort to identify it; he moves his vision a slight degree on either side of the suspected object. For some medical reason, far too deep for me, a person is, at times, able to establish there is an object present and sometimes identify it.

Duties for some crews on Pathfinders were varied, depending on the target and the composition of the raid. On the night of 30th of March 1944, my legitimate 20th birthday, we were sent to Nuremburg as a 'backer-up.' We were loaded with target markers and flew in the centre of the main force bomber stream. When the raid was in progress, we took directions from the master of ceremonies who circled above us and the target, giving instructions on resetting the markers to bring the stragglers or late arrivals back on the aiming point. While flying towards the target, we began to see many exchanges of gun fire and aircraft going down in flames. Our duty was to report the incidents to our navigator for plotting on his charts; however, they were happening so fast he said he could not keep up. We had earlier spotted a Lancaster about five hundred feet below and off to our starboard, cruising along at the same speed as ourselves. Suddenly it burst into flames, illuminating us and the fighter that had just hit him, a Me110 night fighter just below the Lancaster and it was following the Lancaster on its final slow descent. I suggested to Mac we alter course to port to get away from the brilliant light of the burning aircraft, and he did. We sighted many other such exchanges that night that indicated to us that Bomber Command was taking a beating. This was my birthday and here I was at 18,000 feet over Germany, in the rear turret of a Lancaster, making a grand entrance into my twentieth year amidst absolute mayhem. After we had our turn over the target and headed for home, we saw nothing further.

Upon interrogation all crews realized that those in the front of the raid saw no activity from enemy fighters, but those in the centre of the bomber stream had received it all. The following morning the B.B.C. announced that Bomber Command had lost 95 aircraft as the result of enemy action. This number did not include those who had got back to England and crashed for various reasons. 665 airmen from the Commonwealth and England were reported missing in one single raid, one bombing raid I will never forget, as it had a profound effect on me later. Much has been written about this particular operation, but by far the most researched document in my view is the book *The Nuremburg Raid* by Martin Middlebrook, 1973, printed by Allen Lane, Penguin Books, London, England.

My brother Jim had arrived in England and was stationed with a Canadian bomber squadron in 6 Group near Leeds, Yorkshire. I spent only one leave with him in Leeds. As a commissioned officer it was difficult for me to stay on his base, as I had no civilian clothes, so I could not stay in his barracks or eat with him in his mess. During this leave Jim approached me about starting up a business back home in Mission after the war. He said we would have some gratuities coming upon discharge which would give us the necessary finances. He had worked it out roughly and said I would have about $1500 and he would get nearly $700. I was a bit upset that he had calculated my gratuity without even talking to me first. However, the subject died and we went on to enjoy our leave. I tried to get him to join me next leave on my station but this fell flat. I did not see him again until I returned from overseas.

The country roads in rural England in 1943 became locations for the erection of a large number of camouflaged quonset huts. Most of them were open both ends, others were closed in and secured. These huts were full of crates, boxes and equipment. We assumed they were in preparation for the pending invasion, as England had become one giant airfield and arsenal. When we started bombing French, Belgium and Dutch transportation facilities, we noticed at the same time these huts were being emptied. This was a sure sign the invasion was not that far off.

April, 1944, was the start of the raids into Holland, Belgium and France as part of the softening up process for the pending D-Day invasion. We attacked railway yards, canals and any other transportation facility. Although these trips across the English Channel were short, three to four hours' duration, our losses were high. Some brilliant idiot in Royal Air Force Headquarters decided, as these raids were short, air crews could count only one-half point for each trip toward their totals for a complete tour.

When we started a second tour we were allowed to quit after twenty operations, or go on to thirty. At that figure a rest period was mandatory. Counting each trip as half a point would have compelled us to double the number of trips to complete our second tour. This new regulation considerably reduced our chance of survival. In view of this development, our crew had lengthy discussions to decide what we were going to do. At this juncture I decided to quit operational flying when I had completed my twentieth trip and relinquish my position as rear gunner of Jack McDonald's crew. The others decided to carry on and finish thirty trips under the new rules. Not many months after the rules were changed to count each sortie as a half point, they were rescinded, as H.Q. realized the losses during these short trips were as high as or higher than the long trips into Germany.

I did not reach my decision easily, as we had been together for 3½ years and had worked as a team through many ordeals. We had been shot at continually and in some instances crew members were hit. We had survived injuries and wounds, engine failures, aircraft explosions, fires and crash landings, not to mention numerous near-collisions and other horrendous situations which would cause your faith in survival to waver a bit. We had to be constantly alert to becoming too complacent and developing an attitude that we were invincible. We witnessed other crews succumb to this fallacy; they were no longer with us. We had become an extremely close group of seven men and my decision was about to alter this close relationship.

I had no doubt, however, that my operational experience was starting to show on me. Since the beginning of 1944, I had been waking in the morning to find the bed wet. This was not an isolated incident; it was happening frequently. I had not wet the bed since I was a youngster, but what was happening to me now was a constant humiliation particularly in a hut with thirteen others. I had heard of some going through this trauma, but not within my own group. I found also I was becoming short-tempered and having to apologize for my actions. Neither of these situations was normal, and I faced the fact that my operational duty was beginning to affect my nerves. I had told my skipper Jack McDonald of my dilemma several months before on deciding to terminate my second tour. He had tried to convince me to stay on for the thirty trips and also added that I had been recommended for the Distinguished Flying Cross. I said that I really did not care as I had had enough. We discussed the coming of D-Day and he wanted me to be part of it. Although neither of us knew the date, Bomber Command's activities indicated it was going to be imminent. My D.F.C. came through even though I had put in for transfer and my parents received the following letter from The Minister of National Defence for Air, The Honourable Charles G. Power:

> "I am writing to say how much all ranks of the Royal Canadian Air Force join me in warmly congratulating you and your family on the honour and distinction which have come to your son Flying Officer Jack Denison Routledge D.F.C., through the award of the Distinguished Flying Cross for great gallantry in the performance of his duty while serving with Number 405 Squadron (Pathfinder Force) Royal Canadian Air Force. This officer has completed many successful operations against the enemy in which he has displayed high skill, fortitude and devotion to duty. The personnel of the Force are proud of your son's fine service record."

Meanwhile I was moving closer to completing my final 20 operations. On March 18/19, 1944, we bombed the railway marshalling yards at Tergnier: 171 aircraft — 6 were missing. On April 20/21 we bombed the railway yards at

Lens, France: 175 aircraft – 1 missing. On the 24th of April, 1944, I flew my 51st and last operational bombing raid to Karlesruhe, Germany: 637 aircraft – 9 missing, 3.0 percent of the force.

My former crew carried on, completed their thirty trips and participated in the heavy air activity on D-Day and the invasion of Europe. Did I have any regrets about quitting? The answer is yes and no. Yes, because I had left a fine group of fellows and sure, I wanted to be part of D-Day. No, because my system could not have taken much more. I feel I made the right decision.

While on 49 Squadron, many of us attended the station dances. Here I had met an English girl from the Women's Auxiliary Air Force (WAAF), who was employed on the station as a PBX Operator (Telephone). We would meet in the canteen and drink tea and talk. As she worked shifts and my hours of flying were so erratic, we did not meet that often. Later she was moved to 3 Group Headquarters at Bawtry in Yorkshire. On some leaves I would meet her in Bawtry. On one of these occasions, I asked her to marry me and she accepted. I went to her parents' home and met her mother, father and brother. Plans were made for the wedding in June, 1943, with her brother as best man. After the wedding we parted to our separate stations. Thereafter we spent all my leaves at her parent's house. When my tour ended we planned to make our home in British Columbia. Her brother joined the R.A.F. as a gunner. After training he was posted to a squadron flying Sterling bombers and was later posted as missing; neither the aircraft nor any of the crew were ever found. His name is inscribed in the Runnymede Memorial overlooking the Thames River, where over twenty thousand missing airmen with no known graves are honoured.

After my second tour of operations with 405 Squadron had ended, I elected to extend my stay in England for a while, as my wife had become pregnant and then gave birth to a son. She obtained her release from the R.A.F. and resided with her parents. We discussed our return to Canada many times, but the birth of the baby and the loss of her brother had undermined her resolve.

I was transferred to 29 Operational Training Unit (O.T.U.) at Bruntingthorpe as a gunnery instructor. The chief instructor assigned me to flying instructing. This job meant taking new gunners in the air in old Wellington aircraft, to shoot at drogue targets. Drogue is a sleeve target towed behind another plane and the new gunners would take turns firing at it from the rear turret. I felt I was being treated unfairly as I was a fully qualified instructor, having obtained a Gunnery Leader status with high marks. I had previous experience as an instructor and had just completed two tours of operations. The training officer wore First World War ribbons and an observer's wing which he had probably earned hanging in a balloon basket over France in 1917. He talked to me as if I were just out of training. He advised me his decision stood, and he closed with the comment, "There is a war on, you know." In response I became equally sarcastic: "I had heard there was." I also told him I was not going to fly in worn out, beat up old Wellingtons. He said he was going to have me charged for refusing to fly, and I advised him to go ahead. I heard nothing more of this incident, and eventually a transfer came through to number 82 O.T.U. at Ossington. Just before I left Bruntingthorpe, the long-awaited D-Day and the invasion of France was taking place and everyone was praying for success.

I arrived at Ossington and shared a room with another Canadian air gunner, Stan Hodges. We got along well and exchanged our experiences. He advised me that the chief instructor on this base was also a bit of a nasty person and to watch myself, as he had caused others a lot of grief. I went through the same nonsense with this fellow as I had with his counterpart at Bruntingthorpe. He finally said he was going to have me transferred, and did.

I was sent to the Air Crew Allocation Centre (ACAC) at Bracla, Scotland, very near Elgin. Your past record determined your category. My priority was high having completed two tours of operations and one tour of instructing. After several weeks I was posted to the Royal Canadian Air Force Repatriation Depot at Warrington, Lancashire, put on the staff of the Air Crew Reselection Board and promoted to Flight Lieutenant. The board consisted of five officers and a chairman. All members had served one or two tours on either fighters or bombers. The chairman was Wing Commander 'Buck' McNair, a highly decorated fighter pilot who excelled while in Malta and then flew sorties over the Channel into France. On one occasion his Spitfire caught fire, and he was forced to bail out over the English Channel and received severe burns. Buck was a fine gentleman and a pleasure to work with. Warrington was also the main repatriation point for all Canadian air crew being returned to Canada. As the invasion progressed, the station became extremely busy with the processing of prisoners of war who had been freed by the Allied troops.

Each member of the board was representative of the various flying trades: pilot, navigator, wireless operator, and gunner. Also on staff we had a lawyer from Toronto, a psychiatrist, a medical doctor and a dentist whom I shared a room with. The board's function was to screen all Canadian air crew who had been removed from flying duties for medical or negligence reasons, or for suspected lack of moral fibre. My duty was to interview and to check all documents relating to any gunners referred to us under the guide lines. The inquiries, augmented by reports of interviews by professional staff, were extensive. All documentation was presented to the board at a hearing where the crew member answered questions from the board members and could make a presentation on his own behalf. The cumulative results were used in deliberating this person's future in the air force. In the majority of cases, medical reasons, such as chronic airsickness, colour blindness, heart problems, nervous breakdowns, etc., were cited. All were sent back to Canada with a recommendation for an honourable discharge and accorded all the credits given for service in the air force. Only one person was repatriated with a recommendation for a dishonourable discharge as having been found negligent because of 'Lack of Moral Fibre.' Whether the recommendations were carried out in Canada, I do not know. The board was only a small part of the depot function. All Canadian Air Force personnel serving in the European theatre were required to come through this camp for processing and transportation arrangements. The doctor who was attached to the board was required to go to the various ports and physically inspect all troop transports for sanitation. Returning prisoners of war were given special treatment, as some of them were in very poor physical condition. I was fortunate to meet two former prisoners of war at the depot, whom I had known prior to the time they were shot down.

While at Warrington, I received a circular from R.C.A.F. Headquarters in London advising me that I could qualify for new duties in occupied Germany. As the Allied troops occupied German communities, they wanted to set up immediately a simple government framework. My function as the head of a temporary government would be to organize the utilities, food supplies and any other matter relating to the well-being of the town and its citizens. Following this procedure and as quickly as possible the necessary free elections of city or town councils would take place. The position would remain to supervise the new council for a period of time. It was estimated the appointment would be for a year to a year and a half but I felt this was too long. There were times when I regretted not applying. Years later I met a fellow that did accept the appointment and he said it was enjoyable but tough, as many of the German citizens could not accept the fact their community was occupied.

I was now anxious to return home. My wife was still reluctant to emigrate and our marriage was shaky, but I asked Dr. Ron Easton, the Station Medical Officer, to let me know when a nice ship was available to transport Canadians home. He suggested a ship at Liverpool called the *Athlone Castle*, a very acceptable ship with all its pre-war appointments in place and a former cruise ship operating out of England. I applied immediately and was accepted. I with my wife and son left Warrington on May 1st, 1945, arriving in Halifax two weeks later. Before leaving England, all air crew were asked if they wished to fight in the Pacific. Many did volunteer and others, including me, declined. I just had had enough.

The war in Europe ended while we were with a large convoy in mid-Atlantic. The captain of our liner announced that we would stay with the convoy and practise all safety drills as usual. The German Navy, upon surrender, had ordered all of its U-boats to surface and turn themselves over to the nearest Allied ship. However, the Allied navy did not take any chances by breaking up the convoys or travelling with lights on, as there was some uncertainty as to whether all submarines had received the message, or whether a rogue submarine might ignore the order.

We were the first troop ship to arrive in Halifax after the European armistice. We pulled alongside the dock about 2 p.m. and remained until the following morning. Other than a couple of air force people and the usual dock-workers, there was not a sign of welcome home from anybody. Needless to say, we were 500 disillusioned airmen on the ship. We walked down the gangway the following morning into railway coaches they had brought onto the dock, and left immediately. We all agreed, if Canada ever needed an enema, this was the ideal place to administer it. However, we learned that Halifax had been severely damaged by rioting servicemen celebrating the victory in Europe. A lot of fingers were pointed as various groups were blamed for this fiasco, but no consensus was reached. We now understood why the citizens of Halifax did not want to welcome a shipload of veterans.

We left the train at Montreal and were taken to Lachine base on the south side of the St. Lawrence. Here we were processed for medical, paper work and arranging our transportation home. After two days we were on our way. While on board the *Athlone Castle* I had met another air gunner, Lyle Humphries from Montreal, who also had completed two tours. During our conversations I mentioned I was concerned about subjecting my family to almost four days living in a sleeping car while crossing Canada. By lucky chance his father was a vice president of the Canadian Pacific Railway with his office in the Montreal Windsor Station. After our arrival at Lachine, Lyle arranged a meeting with his father, who kindly obtained a compartment on the transcontinental train from Montreal, Quebec, to Mission, B.C., at no extra charge. Considering all trains were packed solid, this gift was certainly appreciated, as my wife and baby were having a difficult time dealing with the length of the trip and adjustment necessary. The compartment certainly gave some comfort and privacy to her during this long journey towards her new home in B.C.

I was given thirty days' leave and then I was to report to the discharge centre at Jericho Beach in Vancouver for final processing. Two weeks of my leave had passed in Mission when the family received word that Jim was on his way home also. After he arrived, I decided that I would not report to Jericho Beach until he had finished his leave and then we would go together. When I finally reported to the Release Centre, I was immediately asked where I had been. I was given a form listing all the sections I had to visit to be documented, poked, punched and examined before my release. At every office I reported to I was asked where I had been. They all got the same reply. After the doctor, dentist, pay branch, records and many others had completed what was necessary, I was paraded before an administrative officer who was not wearing any wings, but had the rank of squadron leader. We referred to these people as 'wingless wonders.' He proceeded to dress me down for being two weeks late for my processing and for throwing the whole system out of gear and causing numerous other problems. After I had signed and he in turn had affixed his signature on all the necessary forms, he handed me my retirement papers with the comment, "Don't let this happen again." I nearly burst out laughing, but responded, "No sir." This was the 21st of June, 1945, four years and six months after entering the service.

In this period of time I rose from the rank of Air Craftsman Second Class to the rank of Flight Lieutenant and was decorated with the Distinguished Flying Cross, in retrospect, quite an achievement for an air gunner. I often reflect back about my childhood days and why I left home so young. I still do not have any regrets. When I am alone, the experience I had in the air force frequently comes to mind. I can't believe how fortunate I was to survive this conflict when the odds were really stacked against all of us. I have reminisced with other air crew members and they have the same thoughts. I suppose these memories will go with us to our last days.

Chapter 6

Bomber Command

Air Crew Casualties

The air crew casualties quoted hereunder are taken from the book *The Bomber Command War Diaries* authored by Martin Middlebrook and Chris Everitt. These figures are for R.A.F. bomber squadrons operating out of England only.

Approximately 125,000 air crew served in the various squadrons and the operational training and conversion units of Bomber Command during the war. Nearly 60 percent of Bomber Command air crew became casualties. Approximately 85 percent of these casualties were suffered on operations and 15 percent in training and other accidents. The Air Ministry was able to compile the following figures up to May 31st, 1947.

Killed in Action, or died while prisoner of war	47,268
Killed in flying or ground accidents	8,195
Killed in Ground Battle Action	37
TOTAL FATALITIES TO AIRCREW	55,500

Prisoners of war including many wounded	9,838
Wounded in aircraft returned from operations	4,200
Wounded in flying or ground accidents in the U.K.	203
Wounded other than Prisoner of War	8,403
TOTAL WOUNDED	22,644

TOTAL BOMBER COMMAND CASUALTIES   78,144

Runnymede Memorial is situated on high ground overlooking the Thames River near London, England. It was erected in dedication to the 22,000 airmen of the Royal Air Force and the Commonwealth who perished in the European air war and have no known grave. Three thousand one hundred and twenty-five of these are Canadian. Every missing airman has his name engraved in marble plaques facing out on the English countryside and surrounded by gardens.

In 1992, after many years of continuous research, Canadians Les Allison and Harry Hayward published *They Shall Grow Not Old,* a book of remembrance. This is a remarkable biography of over 18,000 Canadian airmen and airwomen killed wherever in the world they served between September 3rd, 1939, and August 12th, 1945. Each entry contains some detail regarding the circumstances at death, make of aircraft and serial number, location of incident, other crew members and burial site. If no burial site is indicated, the person's name appears on the memorials at Runnymede, England; Malta War Memorial, Malta; Singapore War Memorial, Malaya; Alamein War Memorial, Egypt; and Ottawa War Memorial, Ottawa, Canada. This book is still available at Can-Av Publications.

Once I had entered the service I had to learn rapidly, understand the variation in personalities and be able to read the good and the bad in individuals. I was required to accept discipline because it was part of everyday life. I also learned how to do my job to the best of my ability and how to work as part of a team. Operating in isolation, a person may not accomplish much, but as a team, anything is possible. At the risk of sounding egotistical, I am happy with and proud of the accomplishments of our crew and the honour of fighting the war with them. We each respected the others' capabilities and put all our efforts in one direction: to do the job well and, we hoped, survive. We did just that - completed two tours and ended up a decorated crew. We left the Service as close friends and remained that way for many years.

PILOT: Squadron Leader J .R. McDONALD; Distinguished Service Order; Distinguished Flying Cross.

NAVIGATOR: Flight Lieutenant G. G. BELLAMY; Distinguished Flying Cross and Distinguished Flying Medal.

BOMBARDIER: Flight Lieutenant R. W. WRIGHT; Distinguished Flying Cross and Distinguished Flying Medal.

FLIGHT ENGINEER: Flight Lieutenant E.R (Wilbur) WRIGHT; Distinguished Flying Cross and Distinguished Flying Medal.

WIRELESS OPERATOR: Flight Lieutenant J. C. GIBBS; Distinguished Flying Cross.

MID-UPPER GUNNER: Flight Lieutenant T. D. DUFF; Distinguished Flying Cross.

REAR GUNNER: Flight Lieutenant J. D. ROUTLEDGE; Distinguished Flying Cross.

Jack McDonald, Jack Gibbs, Geoff Bellamy and Wilbur Wright went on to a third tour on Transport Command. They flew from England to Corsica, Cairo, and on to Karachi, India hauling supplies. A tour on transport aircraft was calculated by the number of hours flown. They completed the tour and returned home, as did Bill Wright. Geoff Bellamy was still not satisfied and volunteered for a fourth tour with the Tactical Air Group, flying in American-built Bostons in support of the Allied invasion troops in Europe.

I feel it is necessary to insert a post script to this wartime adventure and bring closure to this group whose exploits I have been covering in the last three chapters even though it will be entirely out of sequence in these memoirs.

Wilbur **Wright**, Flight Engineer from Birmingham, England, died of leukemia about two years after the war.

Jack **Gibbs**, wireless operator from Bowmanville, Ontario, worked for the Dowty Aircaft Corporation for a number of years. He became diabetic and died about 1973.

Tommy **Duff,** our mid-upper gunner from Prince Albert, Saskatchewan, remained in the Air Force and was with the first United Nations group to go to Viet Nam when the French were having their problems in that country. He eventually left the air force and became a civilian employee with the R.C.M.P. in Ottawa. While I was stationed in Ottawa, I learned Tommy was working in our Administrative Building and had a serious alcohol problem. I tried to assist in drying him out to no avail. I brought him to our house where he stayed for four days. During this time he had no alcohol and we had a great visit. However, I couldn't keep him all the time and he returned to his own apartment and started drinking again. The R.C.M.P. had to eventually terminate his services. He died a year later.

Jack **McDonald**, our pilot, joined Air Canada after the war and flew out of Vancouver and Toronto for some time. For some reason he quit and took the job as Chief Pilot for McMahon Oil Company in Calgary. He was with this firm for a number of years and we saw each other frequently while I was in Edmonton. He left the oil company and flew for Bradley Air Services in the Arctic and was killed in the crash of a Dehavilland Twin Otter at Frobisher Bay in about 1978. The crash was caused by mechanical failure; the flap on one side broke away just as they were to touch down.

Bill **Wright**, bomb aimer, remained in the air force, attained the rank of colonel and was commanding officer of the Radar Station at Sydney, Nova Scotia. He retired and became office manager for an oil company in Calgary. We communicated and exchanged visits. He died of cancer in Calgary about 1992.

Geoff **Bellamy**, navigator from Canterbury, Kent, went to University in England and obtained his Master's Degree in art and architecture, eventually becoming the principal of this discipline at Canterbury University. We corresponded regularly and Margaret and I paid him a visit in England in 1977. He retired and eventually entered a nursing home where he died in 1997.

To have survived air battles in the dark of night where tremendous losses occurred, I feel our survival was about 25 percent good management and 75 percent good luck. Sadly, my crew fell one by one, leaving me the sole survivor. Over the years I had corresponded and visited with each of them, but I deeply regret we failed to come together as a group after the war.

It is extremely difficult for me to describe all of the very stressful situations we shared together or all of the happy and hilarious times that brought about a very close relationship. In the foregoing chapters I have endeavoured to give the reader an insight into the way of life, tensions, apprehension and tragic situations that transpired during the war. The incidents related leave me prone to criticism as to their accuracy, but I can assure all readers, the accounts given are supported by documentation and others by very clear recall. It is not possible to document each and every incident, as there were plenty that occurred in four and a half years of wartime experiences, particularly when it was over sixty years ago. I, like thousands of war veterans, had to get on with my life in peace-time. The following chapters will relate my struggle to find another identity in this wonderful and turbulent world.

17. Not very often I was allowed out of my cage (rear turret). This was a local flight over England and I was invited up front for a photo opportunity. I am standing behind the pilot. (Jack Gibbs photo)

18. Our crew in Cambridge for a night out. (Jack Gibbs photo)

19. Squadron Leader Jack McDonald D.S.O., D.F.C.
at 405 Squadron Gransden Lodge in 1944.
(Jack Gibbs Photo)

20. One of our dedicated ground crew, an armourer servicing the
rear turret. Note the Removal of plastic leaves the gunner
exposed to the elements but greatly improves his visibility.
(Jack Gibbs photo)

21. Our crew under the wing of LQ-V (Victor) on 405 Squadron (Pathfinders), Gransden Lodge. (left to right) Jack Routledge (rear gunner); Bill Wright (bomb aimer); Jack McDonald p ilot TommyDuff (mid-upper gunner); Geoff Bellamy(navigator); Jack Gibbs (wireless operator); Wilbur Wright (flight engineer). (Jack Gibbs photo)

22. Ground crew doing a last minute check before take-off. The projection
under the wing above the open bomb bay doors is the trailing aerial
outlet. After take-off the wireless operator would let out about 150 feet
of aerial and wind it in before landing. This permitted radio contact
with base when hundreds of miles away.
(Jack Gibbs photo)

23. Photo taken after receiving my Commission in 1944. The eagle
    below the ribbons is the Pathfinder badge awarded only after
    minimum of ten trips with a Pathfinder Squadron. The small
    wing just below the pocket button is the Operational Wing
    awardedto Bomber Command air crew upon completing one
    tour and a bar added for subsequent tours. (RC.A.F. photo)

24. The author being invested with the Distinguished Flying Cross by
Lieutenant Governor Banks at R.C.A.F. Station, Sea Island,
Vancouver B.C. in 1948. King George was unable to make the
presentation as the war had ended and we had been repatriated.
He bestowed this duty on his representative in British Columbia.
(R.C.A.F. photo)

25 & 26.
Refurbished Canadian built Lancaster VR-A dedicated to Andrew Minarski V.C., R.C.A.F. The author took this photo at Kelowna, B.C., while the aircraft was en route from Hamilton, Ontario to the Abbotsford Air Show in British Columbia. This is the only Airworthy Lancaster in Canada. The square on top of the right wing next to the fuselage marks the stowage for a large inflatable 7-person life raft.

27. Post-war picture of Lancaster PM-M2 'City of Lincoln' flying over the City of Lincoln, England, with the land mark Lincoln Cathedral in the background. The cathedral was a familiar sight to thousands of airmen from Bomber Command who flew from bases all around the city. The cathedral has a large stained-glass window dedicated to all who flew during this conflict.

Chapter 7

Back Home Confusion

1945 to 1947

We lived with my parents in Mission and I obtained a job as a trucker for the Mission Fruit Union hauling fruit to Vancouver and New Westminster. I gained some income, but living with my parents was not going well, and I eventually found a small house to rent.

Combining our gratuities from the air force, my brother Jim and I began discussions regarding starting a bus service from Mission, south to Abbotsford and to the Canada-U.S. Border at Huntingdon, plus a second route from Mission through Stave Falls west to Haney, B.C., over the Dewdney Trunk Road. We obtained financing from a firm in New Westminster and we bought two busses. After several hearings, and strong objections from the Pacific Stage Lines owned by B.C. Electric, the B.C. Motor Carrier Branch awarded us operating rights on these runs. However, long hours of driving which Jim and I did caused enormous personal tension and anxiety between us that was compounded because we were losing money. Patronage of our bus service was poor, and after a year I decided to pull out of the arrangement.

My marriage, too, being fragile from the beginning, was deteriorating. These two post-war years were traumatic for both of us, more so for her being a stranger to Canada. Our total incompatibility was a tragic off-shoot of the wartime experience of two young people living on the edge of being alive one day and perhaps dead the next. We talked many times about divorce and always agreed to disagree. I suggested she take a trip to England to see her parents but she refused. Divorce eventually became inevitable. She received custody of the child along with a lump sum of money from me. In 1947 when the divorce was granted we went our separate ways. Shortly after, she remarried.

I had no idea what I wanted to do. I took many jobs: splitting cedar shakes, a carpenter's helper on a construction job, deck hand on the tug boat *Sea Spray* towing log booms from the mouth of the Vedder River down the Fraser River to New Westminster mills. Although I was never unemployed, none of these activities was satisfying. They provided me with income but, needless to say, I was becoming depressed and restless. My personal life was in absolute confusion, all created by my own doing, and it was about time for some serious soul-searching. Moving with such rapidity out of uniform where I had been successful, into the work force, and not knowing what direction to take concerned me deeply. I had many memories of the war but no training for a post-war future. I wanted to change this situation, and a surprise meeting with a childhood friend helped me find the way.

New Year's Eve, 1947, I went to the dance in the Mission Legion with a friend, Nelson Knight, and ran into Margaret Calvert, whom I had not seen since I had left for overseas. During several dances she told me she had graduated as a registered nurse from the Royal Jubilee Hospital in Victoria, B.C. Now living at home with her parents and nursing at the Mission Hospital, she was trying to save enough money to finance a post-graduate course in obstetrics in New Jersey, U.S.A. We began dating regularly and became engaged. I obtained a job of driving bus for Vancouver Island Coach Lines, eventually working out of Duncan, B.C. Margaret and I were married in Vancouver at St. Andrew Wesley Church on July 27th, 1948. Margaret spent her savings on a wedding trousseau instead of her post-graduate course in New Jersey.

Margaret began nursing at the Duncan Hospital. My driving a bus, however, was not a secure living nor were we prepared to accept this work for the rest of my life. One day I pulled into the Duncan depot and met a B.C. policeman whom I immediately recognized as Stan Hodges, the person I had shared a room with at the Royal Air Force Station, Ossington, Yorkshire, in 1944. We immediately struck a close friendship, as did our wives. With Stan, Sadie and Margaret's encouragement, I decided to join the B.C. Provincial Police and wrote my exams under the supervision of Corporal Les Jeeves and Constable George Philips. When my exam results arrived from the B.C. Police Headquarters in Victoria, I was happy to learn I had passed.

The next hurdle was a medical examination. On my medical form my weight was listed at 152 pounds. The requirement for recruits was 165 pounds. I was devastated. However, when I presented the medical form to the interviewer in Victoria, he told me my weight was good enough, as a person's weight has a tendency to fluctuate. After the usual processing, on March 23rd, 1949, I was accepted into the B.C. Provincial Police as a six months' probationary constable.

The police requirements for a birth certificate gave me a few uncomfortable moments. All my documentation for four and a half years' service in the Royal Canadian Air Force showed me as John Dennison Routledge, born on March 30, 1922. The birth certificate I received from British Columbia Vital Statistics listed my birthday as March 30, 1924. This date was no surprise to me, but my names were. I was always under the impression that my first names were John Dennison, Dennison being my mother's maiden name. However, the certificate stated my names as Jack Denison Routledge. Obviously my father had registered my birth, as I know my mother would not have misspelled her maiden name, and I guess he preferred Jack to John.

I was required by the Police Force to secure an affidavit swearing that I, John Dennison Routledge, born on March 30, 1924, was one and the same person shown on the birth certificate as Jack Denison Routledge, born on March 30, 1924. The affidavit was duly sworn by me and witnessed by persons who could identify me. This procedure finally cleared the records and permitted me to get on with my life as the person I am supposed to be.

At this same time, R.C.A.F. Headquarters in Ottawa contacted me to advise an investiture was shortly to be held at the R.C.A.F. Station Sea Island at Vancouver, B.C. The investiture was for the presentation of my Distinguished Flying Cross by British Columbia's Lieutenant Governor Banks. As Stan Hodges received the same call, our wives attended with us in 1948. These investitures are normally carried out by King George VI, but with the war ending and our repatriation to Canada, the duty was bestowed on the King's representative in B.C. I had many reasons to be happy – my wife, Margaret, close friends, recognition of war service, and my new job as a civilian in the police service.

Chapter 8

B.C. Provincial Police & R.C.M.Police

Vernon, B.C.

1949 to 1950

Our first posting was to Vernon, B.C., a town in the beautiful Okanagan Valley in the interior of B.C., an area of lakes and hills and productive orchards and farms. We were thrilled to be embarking on a new life and career. Since the Duncan Hospital would not release Margaret until she had served her month's notice, I went on ahead, rented a small apartment in preparation for her arrival, and became familiar with a new work environment and the city.

The B.C. Police Detachment consisted of one sergeant, one corporal and twelve constables. The sergeant was Leonard Backler and the corporal was John Arthur Knox. I learned very early that Corporal Knox was the boss. The saying was that any person serving at Vernon Detachment came from the "School of Hard Knox." Although this epithet may sound like criticism, in later life we were thankful for his direction and leadership, which served all of us well as we progressed through the ranks.

Margaret arrived in Vernon a month later on the train. As the apartment we had was pretty sparse, we were later successful in   renting a bigger place in the west end of the city. It was a two-bedroom house with a stuccoed exterior spattered with bilious green blobs of plaster. The local citizens called it "the spotted house." The interior, however, was very nice with hardwood floors and other creature comforts and necessities. The large lot had a mature asparagus patch and twenty-five prune trees. At work I shared all shifts with another constable. Margaret began shift nursing in obstetrics at the hospital. The hospital was very short of nurses so they let her work the same shifts as I did just to get her on staff. It was a very good arrangement, which made shift work tolerable for both of us.

On the evening and night shifts, the two constables on duty were allowed only seven miles per shift in the police car. The rest of the shift was foot patrols, checking doors of the business premises and all the alleys. If we found a door unlocked, we were not permitted to leave the premises until we had phoned the owner and he personally attended and checked to see if all was well. Calling the owner out of bed to check his premises increased the probability that he locked his doors each evening from then on. This type of policing certainly gave Vernon one of the lowest crime rates in B.C. communities at that time.

The winter of 1949/50 was extremely severe, but our foot patrols were carried out regardless. The Vernon Fruit Union packing house located in the downtown area had a large thermometer mounted between two poles to ensure accuracy. We would check the temperature several times during the shift and it would be reading – 40 degrees F at 3 a.m. We would have to start the police car every half hour to prevent it from freezing. The fruit farmers suffered severely. It was so cold for such a length of time that thousands of fruit tree trunks were split so wide and deep that a person could place his hand inside. As one could expect there were serious fires that cold winter. Watkin Motors, the Ford dealership, was located one block south of the Kalamalka Hotel. On one shift I noticed a red glow in the window of the body shop and ran to the nearest fire alarm box. The fire department responded quickly and put the fire out. The grateful owner, Joe Watkins, came to the office the next day to say if we had not discovered the fire when we did, the whole premises would have been destroyed. Although Joe Watkin is now deceased, Watkin Motors in Vernon continues and is reputed to be the oldest Ford dealership in Canada.

Not too long after my arrival in Vernon, I experienced my first murder investigation. A Chinese market gardener was murdered by a hired hand named Joseph Ouillette. The market garden was located near Okanagan Landing on what is now called the Marshall Farm. The scene, of course, had to be secured and guarded. I, being the most junior person on the detachment, was selected to sit out on the scene all night and guard the evidence until the Identification Section arrived from Kamloops the following day. Ouillette was eventually arrested in Vancouver and appeared in Vernon Assize Court where he was convicted and sentenced to life in prison.

Vernon's small Chinese community was comprised of Goon Hong's Café, the Lotus Gardens Restaurant, the Chinese Free Masons Hall and a few rooming houses, one of which was Hop Sing's. Drifters would stay here for a day or two and we were required to check the register and the rooms every night shift. One night Howard Turner and I found at the bottom of the stairs a local female passed out from drinking. After we put her in the police car to take her to the cells, Howard took the driver's seat and I was in the back seat with this unkempt woman. As she awoke from her stupor she became amorous grabbing for me saying, " Kiss me, honey" and attempting to paw me all over. Howard just laughed and headed in a direction away from the detachment office. Needless to say, I shouted threats of one day getting even.

Did I get even? Yes, I did. While working with Howard again one evening shift, we received a call from Kelowna Detachment advising that a stolen car was heading in our direction. Parking the police car on a side road leading into the Army Camp south of the city, we waited for the stolen car to appear. In the interval Howard saw a skunk running along a ditch near us and decided it was time for target practice. He jumped out of the police car, pulled his revolver and started firing. He missed on every shot and then the skunk turned and ran at him. He in turn scurried for the police car but I had purposely locked the door. He was fortunate. The skunk thought better of his attack and disappeared. We had a lot of laughs over what could have happened.

Six months after joining the force, I and fourteen other recruits from around the province were sent to the B.C. Police School in Victoria for a six weeks' course. The instructor was Inspector Carl Ledoux. The other attendees were good fellows and fifty years later we still maintain casual contact. Inspector Ledoux had an assistant, Corporal Smith, serving as clerk and disciplinarian. He was a nice guy who tried to make out he was strict, but otherwise he was not too aware. He drove a small English car which he parked in his designated spot outside the school. One lunch break as he was on his usual walk, we lifted the car and placed blocks under the rear axle so that the tires barely touched the ground. After classes he jumped in and attempted to drive away, but the wheels just spun. We all watched from a distance and chuckled at the look of consternation on his face as he tried to figure out what was wrong with his car. I remember a similar look on a C.P.R. engineer when the wheels of his engine spun uselessly in the grease we kids had laid on the tracks. The next morning he announced that he was not amused but had his suspicions of who had done this dastardly deed. Nothing more ever came of the matter.

At the conclusion of the course, those of us from the interior of the province returned home over the new Hope to Princeton Highway which had officially opened the day before. On the day of the opening, the highway claimed its first fatalities. A family from Vancouver attended the ceremonies and were returning home when they missed a curve and went down a steep bank. A Mr. and Mrs. Leggatt and another person were killed. We were shocked to learn the Leggatts were aunt and uncle of Marnie Leggatt, who had trained as a nurse with Margaret and had been bridesmaid at our wedding. The suddenness of death is always difficult to handle.

I returned to working shifts and on one particular night at 3 a.m., Constable Frank Reagan and I pulled a suspicious looking car over and checked the driver. We didn't like his answers to our questions, and upon searching the car we found a large number of new tools hidden in the trunk under blankets. He was not about to tell us where these tools came from so we locked him up on suspicion of break and entering. Early the next morning we received a complaint from a tool salesman that many of his new tools had been stolen. Needless to say, he was one happy person when we informed him of our arrest. Frank Reagan and I received the Commanding Officer's Commendation for outstanding investigation.

Hotels seemed to provide me with a great deal of experience in my new career. The Sutherland Arms Hotel was a large hotel built at Okanagan Landing by the C.P.R. in the 1800s to accommodate train passengers awaiting the stern wheelers to take them down Okanagan Lake. The current hotel operator was Doug Sutherland who with his attractive wife lived in a small house next to the hotel. On one occasion when Howard Turner and I were together on day shift, we received an urgent call advising that a guest had gone amok and was wrecking the premises. We arrived to hear that this fellow was in a room on the third floor. He had thrown a dresser out through the third floor window where it had landed on a car parked below and caused considerable damage. Howard and I proceeded cautiously up the stairs checking each floor. Because Sutherland had turned off the corridor lights to impede the man, our progress in the semi-darkness was painfully slow. Upon reaching the third floor, I took the right corridor and Howard, the left. He had not proceeded far when a door flew open and a nude person leaped screaming onto him. Howard was knocked to the floor, the culprit on top of him with his hands around Turner's throat and Howard was on his back punching him in an effort to break free. I leaped on the assailant in an effort to pry him off, but he was not about to let go. I then reached in my back pocket for my issue billy club and struck him a blow to the side of the head. He immediately let go of Howard, turned to me and said surprisingly, "Don't you ever do that to me again," and he released his grip on Howard's neck. We were able to get the handcuffs on him and wrestled him down the stairs to the police car and into the cells at the detachment.

Investigation revealed he was from a hydro construction gang near Needles, B.C., and had come to Vernon for a week-end of recreation. After drinking large quantities of rum, he had observed Sutherland's wife going to and from her house to the hotel and mistook her for a prostitute. He had called the desk many times for her services, but when he received no response he went on his rampage and caused thousands of dollars in damage. The shock came the following day. The sergeant in charge of the detachment came to the office, talked to the prisoner and concluded he was too nice a person to face criminal charges and released him. Both Howard and I were upset and very disappointed with the outcome as were the operator of the hotel and the owner of the car, who were seeking some sort of restitution from this individual. The culprit was never seen again.

The Vernon Hotel was situated on Barnard Avenue (now 30th Avenue) and was one of the oldest buildings in Vernon. One evening a fire broke out in one of the rooms, and despite the best efforts of the fire department, the building was completely destroyed. There were no injuries or loss of life. Roughly a year later Safeway Stores purchased the property and erected a building on the site of the old hotel. After Safeway had been open for a few weeks, the manager was held up and robbed. The robber was never apprehended, but we were highly suspicious of a shady individual who ran a business on Barnard Avenue a block away. We didn't always get our man.

In 1950 rumours flew around that the British Columbia Provincial Police was about to be absorbed by the Royal Canadian Mounted Police. The news caused a lot of anxiety among the members, particularly the junior married members, as the Royal Canadian Mounted Police policy stated a person had to be single to enlist and could not marry until after seven years' service (later changed to five years).

The candidate must also have at least $1,200 dollars in collateral or cash and be over a certain age. Consequently we married members had some serious concerns as to our acceptance into the Royal Canadian Mounted Police. Over a period of weeks all members of the detachment were sent to Kamloops to be interviewed by R.C.M.P. personnel officers and our fears were put to rest. We were advised that though we were junior members and married, we could still make a career in the R.C.M.Police.

The change-over came on August 15th, 1950, and signalled a big change in policing policy, as their approach was different from the B.C. Police. Five hundred and eighty-five British Columbia Provincial Police became members of the Royal Canadian Mounted Police. I do believe nine members were not accepted for reasons unknown to me. Eventually our new uniforms arrived and we had an R.C.M.P. staff sergeant from Saskatchewan come to assist us in interpretation of the new policy. After a period of time, I was sent to Fairmont Barracks in Vancouver for a six weeks' indoctrination course that covered drill, physical training, law, discipline, scenes of crime investigation, R.C.M. Police policy and many other subjects.

A budget of our finances was very important, as our pay was very low and came only once a month. When the R.C.M.P. had absorbed the B.C. Police, the provincial pay was higher than that of the federal force; as a result our pay was subsidized by the B.C. Government until the R.C.M. Police received a substantial pay raise and then the subsidy was terminated. Credit cards were unheard of and a person was lucky to obtain credit. We did our grocery shopping at the Hudson's Bay store in Vernon. Every item you bought was written in a counter book and you paid at the end of the month. Margaret kept a separate envelope for each of the regular bills, such as, hydro, telephone, etc., and money for these bills was put in these envelopes after the cheque was cashed. We bought our first refrigerator from Bennett's Hardware, owned by W.A.C. Bennett, who eventually became premier of British Columbia.

Meanwhile Margaret and I rented a newer and nicer home owned by Sax Peters on 25th Street not that far from the police office, and we moved from the spotted house. We were enjoying Vernon and the life style. We both worked the midnight shift. Often in the morning we would go to the Sutherland Arms Hotel, rent a small row-boat and go out on Okanagan Lake fishing until noon, then go home to sleep in preparation for the next midnight shift. Our social life revolved around events with other members and wives at which time we established many good relationships that exist to this day.

One evening while on shift with Constable Stan Henswold, I noticed a car racing at high speeds up and down Barnard Avenue, into adjacent side streets, running through stop signs and creating a menace to other traffic. Running to the police car parked on the street, I hopped in, picked up Henswold who was standing on the curb and gave chase. The route led us through city streets and then onto the Kamloops Road, up the Goose Lake Road to what was at that time the city garbage dump. He suddenly stopped, jumped out and took a rifle from the back seat. We got out of the police car, Stan on one side and I on the other, with our revolvers drawn pointing at him, as he had the rifle aimed at me. I ordered him to drop the rifle, which he refused to do. I advised him that one of us would get him immediately if he fired. After several very tense moments he lowered the barrel and I rushed him and took the rifle from his grasp. The rifle was loaded, the clip was full, a round was in the chamber and the safety was off. He was taken before a magistrate for a preliminary hearing and ordered to stand trial before the Supreme Court. William Galko appeared in County Court and was convicted of dangerous driving and two charges of pointing a firearm at peace officers. He was sentenced to nine years in the penitentiary. Both Stan and I thought we were very fortunate that this incident ended the way it did.

When a policeman is on the street every day, a great deal of information from the public becomes available. On one midnight shift I was checking the doors of businesses on the south side of Barnard Avenue. At about 3 a.m, a man stopped me with the story that a fellow with a certain name living in the Kalamalka Hotel in a certain room, a civilian cook at the Army camp, was selling quantities of food from the back door of the cookhouse. I thanked him, contacted my shift mate Howard Turner, and suggested I change into civilian clothes and attempt to arrange a purchase. The plan was to use my own car with Howard following me at a distance to the camp. We marked a five dollar note, copied down the serial number and I went to the hotel room and arranged a deal. Since he was very receptive to making a sale, I drove him to the Army Camp and pulled up behind the kitchen. He went inside and a minute later came out with something wrapped in an apron which he dumped on the seat beside me. I gave him the five dollars and he returned to the kitchen. I then gave Howard a pre-arranged signal and we both entered the kitchen, where he was placed under arrest. We took possession of the five dollars to be used as evidence. Although he entered a plea of not guilty to theft, he was found guilty and sent to Oakalla Prison Farm.

Sometimes crime was found in unlikely places. The wife of a well-to-do resident of Vernon was the cause of some consternation to us. Quite often we were called to the Hudson's Bay store as the staff had witnessed her stealing valuable items. Each time the store declined to lay charges, so after a discussion with the manager, we were promised they would look after the situation. This lady was suffering from kleptomania and was really committing harmless acts in the eyes of management. The store staff then adopted a procedure where they would watch her, record all the items she had taken and then phone her husband. He would immediately go home, retrieve the articles, return them to the store and then go back to work. It was a sensible solution. We were not called again.

The very enjoyable three years of our posting to Vernon came to an end in the summer of 1952 when we were transferred to Williams Lake in the British Columbia Cariboo

Country. Vernon had been a good place to "get my feet wet" in police work. I had been exposed to a variety of situations which would be beneficial in my new posting.

Chapter 9

Williams Lake Detachment

1952 to 1955

Our move to Williams Lake had been triggered by an incident in which a constable in the Williams Lake Detachment had apparently became intoxicated and had committed some act that required disciplinary action and a transfer. I was replacing him in Williams Lake and he was coming to Vernon. The house he was vacating was now available to rent, a great relief to us in easing the move.

Margaret and I were excited about the shift to a smaller detachment and a new experience, as we had never been to the Cariboo country before. In July, 1952, we drove to Williams Lake in our own car followed by the furniture van. The highway from 100 Mile House to Williams Lake was narrow, winding and extremely rough gravel for the whole sixty miles. The locals advised us that the road from Williams Lake to Prince George was exactly the same. The moving van unloaded our furniture onto the front lawn, loaded up the other family's household effects, and then we were moved in. Fortunately, the weather was hot and no rain in the forecast.

Williams Lake, population about 1100 persons, had one paved street, Oliver Avenue; the rest were gravel. Wooden sidewalks with horses and cattle grazing in the vacant lots gave the appearance of a typical cow town. There were two grocery stores, two druggists, three car dealerships, service stations, three doctors, a hospital, three hotels with beer parlors and few other amenities. Williams Lake is situated a few miles east of the Fraser River on what is now called Highway 97, the main north-south route to Alaska. To the west of town the road took you to Riske Creek, Alexis Creek, Anahim Lake and eventually to Bella Coola on the west coast of B.C. To the southwest it brought you to Alkali Lake, Dog Creek, the Circle S Ranch and then the Gang Ranch, which at this time was the largest cattle ranch in

Canada. Travelling east from Williams Lake you went through cattle ranches and lumber companies until the end of the road at Horsefly Lake, where there were hunting and fishing lodges and a fish hatchery. Taking the road to the northeast from 153 Mile House, you travelled the route of some of the Cariboo gold rush days to Hydraulic, Likely, Quesnel Forks and Keithly Creek, to name a few. In fact we were surrounded by a sense of early history.

The Williams Lake economy was split between cattle and lumber. Cattle ranching was very big throughout the area. The Chilco Ranch, Dog Creek Ranch, Circle S Ranch, Alkali Lake Ranch and many others were running very large herds and conducted cattle drives to the stockyards each fall for the cattle sale. The Williams Lake Stampede was also an annual event which brought people from the many native reserves, cowboys, and ranchers from all over the vast area for competition and festivities. The lumber industry ran from very large operations to the very small. About fifteen per cent of the smaller mills were referred to as gypo operations as some of them arrived, set up shop and were gone within months, usually owing a lot in wages and unpaid bills. The large mills, such as, Lignums, Gardners, and Konke Brothers, all contributed a great deal to the economy. We found Williams Lake and area very friendly and hospitable and supportive of the local police. Margaret and I were made to feel most welcome.

The detachment consisted of a sergeant and five constables. I was again the junior constable and was assigned the rural area to police; the others were assigned to the town and worked shifts. I worked night and day, as this was a large area of approximately 8,000 square miles with many investigations to be conducted. A trip to Likely or Horsefly, or the Circle S Ranch (Spencer) at Dog Creek would take a whole day going to and from, never mind counting the time for the investigation that had caused the trip. The compensating factor in these long journeys was the warm reception and assistance I received from the ranchers and mill operators. As an example, there were Mr. and Mrs. Place who operated the Dog Creek Ranch, one of the stage-coach stopping places on the old Cariboo trail where the passengers were fed and accommodated for the night. The Places used the old log hotel as their residence. Mrs. Place, a ballerina in England before marrying Geoffery Place, was very artistic. When you entered the house it was like a fairyland, as she had every room decorated in a different theme. One time I took Margaret along and Mrs. Place pulled out all the stops insofar as hospitality was concerned. She served us a beautiful lunch on fine bone china, then gave us a tour of the house and told us all about her background and that of her husband. Even to this date we still recall this wonderful lady, who has since died. Recently, I was browsing in a book store and found a book written by the son, Hillary Place, covering the history of his mother and father at Dog Creek.

On one occasion when Sergeant Joe Howe was away on holidays, I was in the office when a call came advising a motorist's car had broken down on the Cariboo Highway about ten miles north and the driver, who stated he was a member of the Force, requested assistance. I responded in the police car and discovered Assistant Commissioner C.E. Rivett-Carnac, Commanding Officer of 'E' Division (B.C.) with his wife. I brought them into town to the Ranch Hotel and had the car towed in. The car was a Morris Minor and parts had to be ordered. He decided to wait for the car to be repaired, even though the garage said the parts would take two days to arrive. My dilemma was what to do in the meantime with this high-ranking officer, as commissioned officers in those days did not associate with other ranks. Luckily the C.O. was a very fine gentleman and his wife was charming. I introduced him to the other members and asked him if he were interested in going to Riske Creek with me the next day to investigate some minor complaints. He was delighted to have the opportunity. Margaret and I agreed to invite them for dinner that evening thinking they would not accept, but they did. Needless to say, this event meant panic stations for both of us, as we were unsure about what to have on the menu; however, Margaret served up a wonderful meal and the evening went well. The following day I took him to

Riske Creek and he was very impressed with the Cariboo country. He met the owner and wife of the Riske Creek Lodge and we were served tea. Finally on the second day the auto parts arrived and he was on his way back to Victoria. This two-and-a-half day interlude with the boss was at the time rather nerve-racking for both Margaret and me; however, in retrospect we both enjoyed their company and the novelty of entertaining them.

One winter evening I was sitting in the living-room reading and Margaret was knitting when we heard a noise at the window. I jumped up, threw open the drapes and nearly dropped with surprise, as there stood a horse with his face against the glass staring me right in the eye. I went out and chased him out of the yard. I did mention that Williams Lake was a bit of a cow town.

On a November evening the phone rang with the message that the Bank of Commerce had been held up and the manager shot. All detachment members were alerted. Apparently accountant Don Mars was due to return from their temporary branch at 100 Mile House, and manager Leonard Hellyer had been waiting for him so he could open the vault and put the cash away for the night. Just prior to Mars' arrival as Hellyer was opening the front door of the bank, a person stuck a gun in his ribs and ordered him inside. Shortly after, Mars arrived and walked indoors to be confronted by the gunman. He demanded Hellyer open the vault, but when Hellyer said he couldn't, the gunman shot him in the buttocks and then left on the run. Hellyer was taken to the hospital and treated. We called Quesnel and 100 Mile House detachments for assistance and started tracking this individual, the job made easier by our first skiff of snow. After a full night's search, one of the Quesnel Detachment members spotted someone in the bottom of a creek bed with his shoes and socks off and a small fire burning. When accosted, this person pulled a gun; the policeman fired and the bullet penetrated downward through the shoulder and into his lung. The suspect was taken to the hospital and the bullet removed by Doctors Barney Ringwood and Hugh

Atwood. He was shackled to the bed and his fingerprints sent to Ottawa by mail. Five days later an urgent telegram advised that this man was Joseph Seguin who was wanted in Toronto for the murder of a taxi driver. He was to remain in custody at the hospital for several weeks under constant guard. The magistrate held court in the hospital room and he remanded the prisoner for another seven days as required by law.

At this time we were conducting another investigation for two missing persons, a man and wife by the names of Frederick Joseph and Jean Labrie from a small mill seven miles north of town. We learned Seguin worked at this mill also, had befriended these two people and was the last one to be seen with them. The investigation moved into the Merritt area where the Labries' car was found. Sergeant Wally Todd from Kamloops Criminal Investigation Branch (C.I.B.) conducted a detailed investigation that traced Seguin in Merritt with the missing people, then Seguin went alone to Kamloops where he had tried to sell some of the Labries' belongings and had then returned to Williams Lake. We had no doubt that Seguin had murdered this couple, but we had no bodies and insufficient evidence to proceed any further.

When Seguin had recovered sufficiently, the bank robbery and attempted murder charges were commenced in Kamloops Assize Court, where Seguin was convicted and sentenced to life. The Toronto Police then brought him to Ontario to face trial for the murder of the taxi driver where he was found guilty and sentenced to death. Many months passed as all the appeals were heard. Sergeant Todd went to Ontario and tried one more interview with Seguin in view of his pending death, but he refused to say anything about the missing couple. The day before his sentence was to be carried out, Seguin ingested poison he had concealed on his person and died immediately. This act brought closure to the bank robbery and shooting in Williams Lake and the death of the taxi driver in Toronto, but not to the case of the missing Labrie couple. Their bodies have never been found despite intensive searching of the Williams Lake, Merritt and Kamloops areas.

In 1953 my mother died suddenly of a heart attack in Mission. Margaret and I attended immediately as did other members of the family. My sister Kay and husband Lorne, and their family; brother Jim with Doreen and their two sons from Seattle; sister Dorothy and husband Arnold from Gibson's Landing and my youngest brother, Tom. To me, my mother was the link to my parents. She was the person who helped me in my earlier years, corresponded with me during my years overseas, sent parcels, and greeted me warmly upon my return. My mother was the warm link to my childhood years that has provided me with fond memories.

Two further unhappy events occurred about this time. Constables Tuttle and Grudniski of Williams Lake detachment arrested a man and woman for possession of twenty-two capsules of heroin, and we witnessed the pair go through withdrawal in the cells. I can honestly say I never want to witness a person undergo that ordeal again. It was not a pleasant scenario and this would not be the last of my experiences with drugs, traffickers and addicts.

The second was a call from a ranch at Olchiltree, located on the Horsefly Road about 25 miles east advising the children on the neighbouring farm had been shot and killed by a foster child. As Constable Jack Groves was on his way in from Horsefly, we advised the people to watch for him and flag him down, since we had no police radios at this time. Constable Groves found two children dead by a swimming hole at the back of the farm. Jack gave chase through the bush, found the foster child a mile away, disarmed and arrested him. Investigation revealed the three children had been playing by the swimming hole when a disagreement had developed. Apparently the foster child had walked calmly into the house, picked up a loaded rifle while mother was not watching, returned to the swimming hole and shot the two children. The foster child appeared in Juvenile Court for trial, which dragged on for many months. He was eventually sent to Brannen Lake School for Boys near Naniamo for an indefinite period.

The entire Cariboo country of British Columbia is steeped in Canadian history. Many reminders of the famous gold rush of the late nineteenth century still existed in the Williams Lake area. Fred Bass was an insurance and real estate agent whose office was next door to the detachment. His father-in-law, Mr. Haddock, was one of the original stage-coach drivers on the Cariboo trail and a very interesting person to talk to. He told us he had never been held up and robbed but some drivers were. Miners came in pursuit of gold, and still remained in the back hills at this particular time. We knew their names and locations scattered all over the detachment area. Even though decades had passed, these people still felt the bonanza was just around the corner and they were going to strike it rich. The big problem was to keep tabs on them and check on their welfare, as they lived miles from their nearest neighbour. We managed to keep track through the small local stores and country freight truck drivers, who would notify us of any long absences of these old-timers. Some miners lived away in the bush and would erect a box on a pole at the roadside where they would put the grocery list every two weeks. The local freight truck driver would pick up the order, take it to Williams Lake and have it filled at MacKenzie's store. The driver would then drop the order off at the box on the side of the road on his return trip. The prospector would pay MacKenzie's and the trucking company by cheque for the freight costs. This process went on for years, not just for the old prospectors, but also for the ranchers living in the hinterland.

One such trucking firm was the Niquette Brothers who ran from Keithley Creek into Williams Lake. On one occasion they came to the office and expressed concern that one of their customers has not been heard from for a period of time. Having been given a detailed description of his location, I took one of the other constables and Margaret as a nurse in our panel truck with a stretcher and went to this person's box on a post by the road near Keithley Creek. We followed a trail and after about a mile we came to a cabin in a clearing. We knocked at the door, were told to enter and found the prospector in bed. He said he was paralyzed and had been there for quite a while. We placed him on the stretcher and carried him to the road and then to Williams Lake Hospital. Each day we would check on him to see how he was progressing and on the fourth day we were advised he had got up and dressed and returned to his cabin. We never saw the man again. While in his cabin we had been amazed at the cleanliness and neatness. Bookshelves along one wall were filled with works on ancient history and mythology.

In 1953 we received a great surprise. Sergeant Joe Howe, who was in charge of the detachment, was being transferred to Salmon Arm Detachment and I was to assume command. Needless to say, this appointment shocked a lot of people including me. A very short while later I was promoted to corporal, highly unusual for a member with just five years' service. The local citizens seemed pleased with the turn of events. For every five years of service a member is issued a star to be worn on the right sleeve. My five-year star and the corporal stripes arrived in the same envelope.

The Federal government decided to build a new post office in Williams Lake. Attached to it was a three-storey addition housing the R.C.M.Police detachment; the first floor housed the garage for police cars; the second floor was the office plus the single members' quarters, and the third was the living quarters for the member in charge. We were extremely pleased to get new quarters, as our office and cells in the courthouse were very cramped. However, the person who designed the new building obviously had not consulted with the police as to the eventual layout of their portion. All extremely intoxicated people had to be carried up two flights of stairs to the cells. We eventually came into possession of a fold-up stretcher which we carried in the van, and which greatly assisted us in manoeuvring up the stairways.

The U.S. Air Force operated the North American Air Defence (N.O.R.A.D) radar station at Puntzi Mountain, located about 125 miles west of us in the Chilcotin Country.

They had a single engine Beaver aircraft used for commuting to Williams Lake. Whenever the commanding officer was in town he would pay us a visit. He asked that any of his personnel who committed violations of our laws be treated the same as any citizen. He further asked to be notified so he could attend any trial and be provided with any documentation. There was one incident that comes to mind.

Even though I was in charge of the detachment, on Saturday nights I would patrol the community with the member on duty. We were at a dance looking on and making sure all was peaceful when a local youth came to tell me there was a car parked up the street where a fellow had showed him a gun he wanted to sell. I went out to find not far from the hall an old model Buick with New York licence plates. I opened the passenger door, sat beside the driver and asked him to show me the gun. He reached under the seat and produced a .45 calibre automatic that I immediately removed from his possession. He explained he did not know it was any offence to possess small arms. He was senior sergeant in the U.S. Air Force and he was advised that he was under arrest. We searched the car and in the trunk we found two large, heavy duty electric motors with U.S. identification on them. The following day his commanding officer attended court. The sergeant was given a nominal fine, the weapon seized and the accused turned over to the commanding officer and taken back to base. I was advised that he was repatriated to the United States immediately and charged with theft of government property. The mutual friendship had paid off.

Williams Lake had its own local talent in brothers Felix and Bill Konke who were not only mill operators but also professional wrestlers who would be out of town for a few months at a time on the wrestling circuit. When they were home, once a year they would bring in some friends and put on a show at the Legion Hall for the community. These wrestling matches were staged just as you see now on television, with all dramatic hoopla and staged threats to their opponents. The wife of one of the brother's, was a show unto herself. A quite large woman, she would go through the theatrics of screaming and shouting at the so-called opposition and make a few attempts to climb under the ropes to get at them. The locals loved this type of entertainment. Felix told me one day that he and Bill had gone to a wrestling school to learn how to fake their appearance and actions as brutal. The same thing happens today; however, like boxing I am still not impressed with wrestling.

During the Cariboo gold rush, the town of Barkerville, some miles east of Quesnel B.C., boasted a population of over ten thousand and bragged it was the largest city west of Chicago. In the same era, Quesnel Forks claimed its population was nearly seven thousand, many of whom were Chinese who had left railroad work to prospect. This community was situated seven miles from Likely at the confluence of the North Fork of the Quesnel River and the main Quesnel River, at the end of the road.

The buildings in Quesnel Forks, although dilapidated, still had the resemblance of their original purpose. The B.C. Police cells had the bars still in the windows, the Chinese Freemason building still bore a shabby sign as did an old grocery store. The remaining buildings other that a few cabins, were piles of rotting wood.

When I was there, the population of Quesnel Forks was two; one an Oriental and the other a Caucasian, both old prospectors from the gold rush. Likely to Quesnel Forks was a heart-stopping experience, as the road was carved out of the bank high above the Quesnel River. It was constantly caving in and we were forced to make minor repairs to the road just to get by. We regularly visited these two old miners, who lived separately, to check on their well being. One day the Caucasian died and we removed the body to Williams Lake. As he died in-testate, we took the government agent Jesse Foster, to the scene, where all valuables were listed, witnessed by us and taken custody of by Foster on behalf of the Government of B.C.

In the winter of 1953-54, Wesley Speed, the operator of the hotel and store at Likely, called to advise that the Chinese prospector Wong Kuey Kim had been found dead on the Quesnel Forks Road. We attended and found him lying face down and frozen solid in the snow. There was no sign of foul play. We removed him to Williams Lake where an autopsy indicated he had died of a heart attack. The government agent was taken to the scene and looked after the valuables. At this juncture Quesnel Forks population was zero. While writing of this incident in 1999, I had occasion to see a magazine article in the waiting room of the Vernon Jubilee Hospital about back-packing in remote communities. It mentioned the Wong Kuey Kim incident in which the author embellished the account with falsehoods. It states that Wong Kuey Kim had been consuming rum this winter day and when the body was located, a bottle of rum was lying beside him, and so he must have died happy. In fact, the deceased had not consumed any liquor and no bottle was found next to him, as this person did not drink. The autopsy had established that he had died of natural causes. Such irresponsible writing warps our true history and heritage.

A book published by a friend, Irene Stangoe of Williams Lake called, *Cariboo-Chilcotin,* Pioneer People and Places, touches on the historical aspects of various communities throughout the Cariboo, and area put a true perspective on the history of this region.

Several months after Wong Kuey Kim died, Wesley Speed and a friend drowned in the Quesnel River when their boat capsized while they were attempting to move it up the rapids into the Quesnel Lake while the river was at flood stage. The irony of this accident is it occurred right in front of his hotel at Likely. Speed's body was never recovered; the other was found lying in the rocks on the shore near Quesnel Forks.

As a post-script to the community of Barkerville, the old town was declared a heritage site and over the years has since been restored to near its original state. It is now a summer tourist destination where the old stores and saloons are open, and the dance halls have been activated along with the old Court House where actors portray the famous Judge Begby, the "Hanging Judge." The town now truly provides all of us with a glimpse into our history of the gold rush era of the 1800s.

Baron Von Reidermann was a kindly man, who with his family had fled Austria in 1939 just prior to Hitler's occupation of that country. The Reidermanns were shareholders in Standard Oil Company of New Jersey. Upon their arrival in Canada the family bought a large ranch at Alkali Lake, about twenty-five miles southwest of Williams Lake on the Dog Creek Road. During my travels in the area, I would call upon them, as I did with most of the ranchers. He became very friendly and would assist us in any way possible when required. When in town he always called at the office to extend his greetings. Some years after our departure from Williams Lake, Baron Von Reidermann died and his son took over running the ranch. One Hallowe'en this son was preparing a fireworks display from a raft on the small lake next to the Indian Reserve. He apparently fell off the raft and drowned, a sad end.

The Pacific Great Eastern Railway (P.G.E.) ran from the coastal town of Squamish north through Williams Lake to Quesnel. The station agent at Williams Lake and his wife were quite the characters, who spent much of their spare time in one of the beer parlours associating with some very questionable individuals. During a routine check of a car near 150 Mile House, we found three really rough types, and further checking through the car brought to light a large sum of money hidden under some papers on the back floor. They refused to tell us where it came from but Garnet Marks, one of the three, said it was his. Since we had no authority to seize it, we let them go. Several hours later the station agent complained Garnet Marks had robbed him. While in the beer parlour the agent apparently had given Marks his pay cheque to be cashed at the bank and returned to him. Instead Marks took off with the money. Not knowing the circumstances, we had found the money earlier but let Marks go. We located the suspects again, the money still in the car, and all three were arrested. However, it was the last the station agent saw of his money until the court trial. The County Court judge found Marks guilty and sentenced him to eight years in prison.

Jamieson Construction was working in the Williams Lake area under contract to the P.G.E. to build a new trestle roughly five miles north of town. A temporary siding was built at the site, and a work train consisting of a full cook car, bunk cars and usual equipment cars were parked there. Jamieson reported to the office that over the week-end his cook car had been broken into and a large commercial refrigerator stolen. Many months passed but we were unable to come up with any suspects. One day a fellow walked into the office, asked if we were still looking for the refrigerator, and advised it was located at McCleese Lake, north of Williams Lake. He named the suspect and told us that it was buried in this person's back yard. Then he drew a plan of the house and lot and marked where the fridge was. We obtained a search warrant and served it on the suspect, who denied any knowledge of the case. We then went to the location as shown on the map and after two scoops with a shovel hit the top of the refrigerator. The suspect was shocked as to our accurate knowledge. He asked how we knew but he was never told. I am sure he felt he had been double-crossed by some of his friends. He had ample time to do some thinking, as he was sentenced to three years.

The Cariboo had many colourful characters, one of whom was Judge Henry Castilou. This gentleman had been raised in the Cariboo country and knew all the old-timers and the folk lore that went with them. The Judge had been appointed at the County Court level; he resided in Williams Lake but travelled throughout the area holding court. Henry was a very large man with a booming voice that could be heard all over the building when he was presiding. We had a case of forgery where the man was arrested on the street just after passing a bad cheque in a grocery store. Forgery charges could not be heard in Magistrates Court, so the culprit asked to waive the preliminary hearing and appear in County Court as soon as possible. His request was passed on to the Clerk of the Court, Jessie Foster. She contacted Judge Castilou and he consented to the trial the following day with my acting as prosecutor. This fellow pled guilty and after his past record was read into the court, Judge Castilou boomed out, "I sentence you to eighteen months in Oakalla Prison Farm." While the prisoner was being taken downstairs, he commented, "I bet all my buddies in the Lakeview Hotel beer parlour must have heard the verdict."

Judge Castilou resided in a home over looking Williams Lake. One day he phoned that a deer was down on the ice andbeing harassed by two dogs. We responded with rifles and found the pitiful sight of a deer on its side, two dogs leaping on it continually and taking bites out it. We each took aim at the dogs and fired simultaneously and both dogs instantly went down. The deer was unable to stand because of a broken leg. The scene was approximately 300 yards out on the thawing ice, making it too dangerous for any person to venture onto it, so we therefore put the animal out of its misery. Since we could not reach the dogs to establish their identity, they and the deer were left waiting for the ice to thaw completely. The next day a woman appeared at the office accusing us of shooting her dog which, according to her, was a prize-winning Dalmatian. We admitted we had shot the dogs, one being a Dalmatian. She stated she was going to sue us, so I read the sections from the Provincial Game Act giving us the authority under these circumstances to shoot these dogs. I further advised her that County Court Judge Henry Castilou had contacted us, and we had responded as we would to any complainant. She stormed out of the office and nothing further ever came of this incident.

At one time there was a major crime that we referred to as "The Clothesline Bandit." For weeks women's under-garments were being stolen from various clotheslines during the night. The local ladies were becoming concerned that it was some "pervert." We did not have any clues or suspects but the complaints kept coming in. One noon hour the principal of the high school called to report a young fellow in a pick-up truck doing wheelies and burning up rubber in front of the school. He was obviously trying to impress the young girls eating their lunches there. Constables Pethick and Wreggett responded, arrested the fellow and brought him and his truck to the office. We searched the pick-up and found women's underwear stuffed in the glove compartment, under the seat and down behind the seat, as well as in a wooden box on the back. Obtaining a search warrant, we went to his parents home in Marguerite, approximately twenty-five miles north. The members were astonished with what they found - piles of underwear under the bed, behind the dresser and in all the dresser drawers. The mother of this nineteen year old was equally surprised and said she had no idea what he was doing.

Our problems had now just begun. The suspect stated he was going to plead not guilty and wanted a lawyer, which was arranged. We contacted all the persons who had complained, as we now had two very large boxes of underwear to be identified, and the women would be required to appear in court to testify as to ownership. At this stage we ran up against resistance. Only one woman appeared at the office and identified her panties from some needlework initials she had done on the leg. She was adamant that these panties were hers, she was ready to testify, and she hoped to get this fellow with the perverted mind off the streets. The lawyer appeared at the office and he was informed that we had positive identification and were ready to proceed. I did not tell him how many people had identified their clothing. He called several days later, said he wanted his client to plead guilty and asked me for a court appearance as soon as possible. The young fellow was given six months and recommended for psychiatric evaluation. I often thought how close this suspect came to being free, had it not been for a determined young lady who was not the slightest bit embarrassed to testify. In typical small town fashion, this case had the chins wagging for many months and generated many jokes. Oh, yes, all the unclaimed underwear was eventually burned.

The Force had a DeHaviland Beaver aircraft float plane stationed at Vancouver. The pilot was Staff Sergeant Stan Rothwell and the engineer was Special Constable Ray Cormier. On many occasions we requested their services to search remote lakes for missing persons. Some were very large lakes such as Chilco, Horsefly and Quesnel. During my tenure at Williams Lake there were several drownings in Quesnel Lake, which had the infamous reputation of never giving up a body. The temperature in this glacier-fed lake was extremely cold and prevented gases from forming in the bodies and floating them to the surface. Many times we called for Stan Rothwell to come to Williams Lake and pick up a member to search the area where the drowning had taken place. As a result we became stalwart friends.

On one occasion Alexis Creek Detachment, seventy-five miles west of Williams Lake, called to advise that a six year old native boy was missing from his home in the remote area of the Chilcotin referred to as the Chezzicut. As there were no roads, Constable Bob Turnbull requested the plane to fly him into this region with his saddle and other gear. He would be let off at the lake side village where he would rent a horse. Rothwell arrived without Engineer Cormier, as the plane was to be loaded with riding equipment. We picked up Turnbull and all his gear and flew him to Ootsa Lake located about 60 miles northwest of Alexis Creek. There he met the families, outlined his search plan and received their co-operation. He informed us he would be back at Alexis Creek in about two weeks.

He also asked us to do an air search of the area around this lake and several others before returning to Williams Lake. As we circled one lake looking for any signs of the young child, we noticed an old building on the lakeshore, so we landed out in deep water and taxied slowly towards land, watching for rocks and sunken logs. About three hundred yards away we slowly came to a stop. We found we had run aground on a mud bank. The water was so clear it gave the illusion of being a few feet below the floats but in reality was about four inches. We each got on a pontoon and tried unsuccessfully to paddle the aircraft backwards through the same tracks we had made in the mud. After several hours of exhausting labour, we managed to move enough mud from around the floats to allow the aircraft to swing a bit at a time under its own power until we had lined up with tracks we had made coming in and reversed our route out of the mucky mess. Once we were airborne again, Stan Rothwell and I could joke about the anxious hours we had spent trying to get this beast free of the mud. I said to Stan, "Can you imagine writing a letter to the commissioner advising him that one of his DeHaviland Beavers is sitting gracefully in the mud on a remote lake about one hundred and fifty miles northwest of Williams Lake where there is no road access?" We knew there were two cardinal sins in the R.C.M.Police: one was to lose a prisoner and the second to lose an exhibit. Losing an aircraft in this manner would definitely have headed the list!

Unfortunately, the lost boy was never located. Constable Turnbull and the search party scoured the area for a week, and he arrived back in Alexis Creek on schedule. All believed the young lad was the victim of bears.

The district engineer for the Department of Highways came to the office one day to complain that the manager of the Red Jacket Lodge and his wife were blocking the road that ran by their place on Horsefly Lake. He said they were under the impression that half the road allowance really belonged to them. He had attempted to show them the right-of-way but had been ordered off their property. He asked me to visit them explain the consequences of their action, as Highways had to get on with the widening of this road. Several days later I met the owners and explained why I was there. They greeted me warmly. I had a copy of the plans, and after the meeting they said they had no problem with widening the road and for the department to go ahead. The problem they had was not with the district engineer, but the foreman who, in their view, was pretty high-handed in his attitude and actions. Several weeks later I dropped in to see how they were doing. They greeted me like an old friend and after serving a cup of tea we parted. Whenever possible, while in the Horsefly area I would stop in to visit them and there was no doubt they liked that very much and always put the kettle on. The road work was completed without any further problems.

In April of 1955, we had very sad news from Burnaby where Margaret's parents had bought and shared a home with her brother Tom, his wife Jean and their four children. They advised Jean had died suddenly of hemorrhagic staph pneumonia. After the funeral service a family discussion was held. Margaret's mother was about to depart on a six months trip to England and her homeland of Scotland, and her father was to come to live with us in Williams Lake until her return. Tom was to leave shortly for an aeromechanics' duty in Hong Kong and Tokyo with Canadian Pacific Airlines. It was decided that they go ahead with their plans and the children would be placed with relatives and friends in the interim. Patti (Patricia Dianne), the baby, aged fifteen months, came to live with us. Margaret's mother was to look after the other children upon her return, but at age 67 she could not handle the baby. This arrangement carried on for the next few years and we later adopted Patti as our own.

The members of Williams Lake Detachment, six in all, put in tremendously long hours every day. There was no such thing as overtime, and getting a day off was almost a privilege. Five of the constables were single men and lived in barracks within the detachment. Despite the long hours not one complained; they were happy to work, as everything was a learning experience. These members were rotated to other detachments on a regular basis. I might add that many of them rose through the ranks to senior N.C.O.s or commissioned ranks in later years. Superintendent Wonnacott, my commanding officer from Kamloops, said during one inspection, that he was recommending me for a transfer, as I also needed a rest.

Both Margaret and I had mixed feelings about leaving Williams Lake, as during these three years we had made many friends. On the other hand, I was looking forward to a change of pace. Originally I was selected to go to Kelowna Detachment, but the appointment was changed, as a corporal with an asthmatic son who needed the area's climate was selected on compassionate grounds. Instead I was posted to North Vancouver Detachment as a shift N.C.O.

These prospects were anticlimactic, as they did not interest me much, but we prepared for the move. Doctor Barney Ringwood and his wife Gwen, a playwright and author, hosted a tremendous farewell party for us. There were speeches, skits, food, presentations and of course the usual liquid refreshments. I received letters from citizens, including Mr. Mario Reidermann, wishing us well on our transfer and thanking me for the assistance rendered over the years. All of these people will forever live in our memories. Margaret, I, Patti and Grandad left for North Vancouver in August, 1955.

28. Margaret and I on our
honey moon. 1948

29. Dressed in B.C.
Provincial Police
uniform at Vernon, B.C.
1949.

30. A serious fire on my shift , the Vernon Hotel burned to the
ground within a few hours. There were no casualties

31. Royal Canadian Mounted Police
dress uniform, 1951. Note the white
lanyard.

32. Williams Lake Detachment dressed in red serge jackets. Photo taken outside the old detachment building and Provincial Court House. Sergeant Joe Howe, Constables Jack Routledge, Gordon Rasmussen and Jack Groves. (1953)

Chapter 10

North Vancouver Detachment

1955 to 1956

The move to North Vancouver came as a bit of a shock, as we had developed a small town attitude over the years. We had a great deal of difficulty in finding a home but eventually did locate one very close to Lynn Creek. The yard was overgrown with long grass and weeds and alive with garter snakes and slugs. Needless to say, we were not the happiest people in the area, but we were determined to stick it out and hoped to find better accommodation.

My mother-in-law returned from Scotland after we arrived in North Vancouver and Marg's father, after having several small strokes when living with us, died in Burnaby on Boxing Day, 1955. His illness and death saddened us.

My work place on the detachment was supervising shifts and dealing with problems, some serious, most quite mundane. The detachment was split into sections: the Capilano Area, the Lonsdale Area and the Dollarton-Deep Cove Area. The shift had one telephone and radio operator in the office, and one member patrolling in each of the patrol areas, a corporal supervising overall. I would spend most of the shift riding with the members patrolling the three areas, a terribly dull routine after my recent experience in Williams Lake. However I didn't ever voice a complaint to my supervisors. After six months I was interviewed by the Personnel Officer from Victoria, who inquired as to what I was doing. I immediately responded, "Nothing," and likened my job to that of a third class constable. After considerable discussion, he said he was going to have me transferred but at the moment could not say where. Never the less, after being on North Vancouver Detachment for a mere ten months, my transfer came through effective immediately and I was placed in charge of Squamish Detachment. Living quarters for the man in charge were provided, thus eliminating the problem of locating accommodation.

We contemplated this move with no regrets. Arrangements were made for me to make a trip via our police launch *Little Bow* to have a look at the living quarters at Squamish. I was greeted by Sgt. Ted Fleetwood and shown about the building and the town. I returned to North Vancouver that same evening. Sergeant Fleetwood was moving to Trail B.C.,

Chapter 11

Squamish Detachment

1956 to 1960

Squamish is located thirty miles up the coast from Vancouver at the head of Howe Sound and at that time it was accessible only by boat or float planes. Our furniture was transported in a moving van on a barge. We travelled on the old passenger boat and at one time the West Vancouver ferry, the *M.V. Hollyburn,* along with the moving company employees and with our pet cat Sassy in a crate on the deck. It was the summer of 1956 and we were off to our next adventure.

This was Margaret's second sojourn in Squamish. She had resided here in her earlier childhood and had started her schooling at the Mashiter Elementary School. Her father had been a forest ranger with the B.C. Forest Service and her family had arrived in Squamish after a stint in the Queen Charlotte Islands. Consequently, she felt quite at home in our new posting.

She found part-time work as a nurse at the Squamish Hospital and she relates this little anecdote. One of the local Mount Currie native girls became pregnant and was admitted to the Squamish Hospital for delivery. When asked the name of the father, she revealed only that he was one of the Hume and Rumble employees. The birth produced twins and to identify them, because of the lack of information from the mother, the babies were temporarily named Hume and Rumble by Doctor Kindree and hospital staff. These names served well during the short hospital stay.

The major industries were logging, which was very active, and the Pacific Great Eastern Railway terminal point. The main repair shops for the railway that ran from Quesnel to Squamish were located at Squamish and had quite a large payroll. This railway was to become our main source of transportation to move about our detachment area. The only road was from Britannia Mines through Squamish to Brackendale ending at the Cheakumus River, total length approximately twenty five miles. However, there were power line roads along with the many miles of logging roads that wound throughout the entire valley on the mountainsides, all leading to the log dumps on Howe Sound. About six or seven logging firms had been established in this area for many years, and their owners and operators were all active members in the community. The manager of Empire Mills when we arrived was the mayor of Squamish. Pat Brennan was another logger who with his partner John Drenka owned the Howe Sound Timber Company. Pat later became the mayor of Squamish and over the years we became close friends.

The detachment consisted of a corporal and four constables, three of whom were single. Our policing responsibility included Britannia Mines, Woodfibre, Alta Lake and all points north to Pemberton and on to D'Arcy. Woodfibre was a pulp mill and company town situated on the north side of Howe Sound and only accessible by boat. As we had no water transportation, the manager of the Woodfibre plant gave us access to the company tug boat any time we wished to go to Woodfibre. We just phoned the company office.

Similarly, Superintendent Harry Nicol of the Pacific Great Eastern Railway arranged for us to call the dispatcher for transportation on any train, freight or passenger, to any destination from Squamish to D'Arcy at no charge. Policing of Pemberton from Squamish was carried out entirely by rail. We had a member stationed at Pemberton on a two-week rotation. I would dispatch a single member to Pemberton by rail, usually a freight train, where we rented a room at the Pemberton Hotel that also served as an office and living quarters. We rented another building to house a cell for prisoners. We used a four-wheel drive panel truck to get to Mount Currie, one of the largest native reserves in British

Columbia, and also to D'Arcy. A provincial magistrate had been appointed for the Pemberton area.

Mount Currie Indian Reserve had its own general store. One afternoon the owner reported that he had been broken into by one of the locals, who had mounted a horse and galloped off into the woods. Our member at Pemberton responded to the call, borrowed a horse from one of the ranchers and took after the suspect, riding bareback. After a fast pace through the trees, the horse decided to turn for home at the gallop. The policeman could not change the horse's mind nor slow it down. They arrived at the stable, and when the horse came to a large pile of frozen manure, it suddenly stopped and the rider catapulted over the animal's head and landed face first into the frozen pile. He suffered total eradication of the brass buttons from his uniform and frozen manure was imbedded into the weave of the fabric. He had scrapes to his face and hands but was otherwise not seriously injured except for his ego and dignity. He phoned me in Squamish to advise me of the robbery and the riding event. I advised him to hop on the next southbound freight train and another member would be sent immediately. When he arrived at the North End Freight Yards, I must say he was a sorry looking mess. His narration of the incident of course brought howls of laughter from all, but he could not see the humour in any of it and was quite indignant. He was fortunate not to have been seriously injured. Ironically, the culprit gave himself up two days later, as he was not equipped to withstand the rigours of another winter night.

The magistrate at Pemberton was a fellow by the name of Kenward who was also an accountant at one of the sawmills. The company complained to us that Kenward had pilfered a considerable amount of money from the mill. We undertook an investigation and found sufficient evidence to charge him with theft. He was arrested on a warrant and placed in custody. Kenward's being the magistrate presented another problem. As the magistrate received all the fines and costs from those who were given time to pay by the magistrate. Our members were prohibited from accepting any fines. However, in those days there were police costs which were assessed for issuing a summons or for arrests which were also paid to the magistrate. He in turn would pass the police costs to us, we would immediately issue him an official cash receipt, and these funds were then forwarded to the Receiver General for Canada. When we arrested Kenward, we immediately conducted an audit to determine if all the fines had been submitted to the Provincial Government Agent at Lillooett and that all the costs had been handed over to the police.

At this point the problems associated with the case escalated. Squamish Detachment for administration purposes was part of Vancouver Subdivision, commanded by a superintendent. When I notified Staff Sergeant Harry Jordan, the Section N.C.O. for my area, he in turn advised the Officer Commanding of the arrest of Kenward and the audit that was being conducted into the fines and costs. Up to this point the investigation and audit was progressing very well. Now the Officer Commanding was on the phone to me every day issuing instructions on how to conduct the investigation and questioning me on how Kenward had got to be a magistrate. I advised him Kenward's appointment was made before my arrival and the selection was entirely in the Provincial Attorney General's jurisdiction. He would not accept this explanation, as he felt I was somehow responsible. His constant instructions and lack of investigation experience nearly drove Harry Jordan and me to distraction, but we agreed we would carry on with the investigation despite his inept interference. We established that all fines had been paid by Kenward to the Government Agent at Lillooett. All the police costs were accounted for except fifty cents. When the Officer Commanding heard about the missing fifty cents, he was outraged and immediately ordered an internal investigation. Practically every day he would phone to admonish me for losing the fifty cents and tell me how disappointed he was in my handling of this matter. I was so fed up with this nonsense I finally offered to pay the fifty cents and write closure. I guess I hit one of his sore spots, as he went into a tirade that my suggestion was an easy way out of an investigation and continued to rant on about my failure to find the money.

In the meantime Kenward was questioned about the missing money and he said he probably had forgot to give it to the constable. He appeared in court for theft of several thousand dollars from the mill and was convicted and sentenced to a term in Oakalla Prison Farm. The member on duty at the time in Pemberton when the fifty cents went missing was Constable Johnson, who had since left the Force and joined the Ottawa City Police. Since Harry Jordan was to attend a Canadian Police College course in Ottawa, the Officer Commanding ordered him to interview Johnson while he was there. Jordan reported that during the interview Johnson denied receiving the fifty cents and was so disgusted with all the nonsense over this paltry sum that he offered to pay it himself! To bring this frivolous investigation to a close, as we jokingly called the "Fifty Cent Caper," the money was never located. The Officer Commanding never did let me off the hook. For months afterwards he constantly admonished me over the investigation always stating how disappointed he was in me. To put this matter into perspective, Harry Jordan and I tried to bring a dollar figure on how much it had cost to find fifty cents and we came up with a conservative figure of approximately five thousand dollars.

Construction of the railway extension to North Vancouver was proceeding rapidly and the building of the highway from West Vancouver to Squamish was being accomplished at the same time. Both these new routes wound their way along Howe Sound from Horseshoe Bay to Squamish, the railway practically at sea level and the highway above, and both were being blasted from the mountainside. The railway was completed first, and there was a grand opening ceremony at Squamish with Premier W. A. C. Bennett and his entourage of local politicians and company brass and, of course, our presence in red serge uniform. Railway freight and passenger service was now running from Prince George to North Vancouver, which brought to reality a long-time dream of many people. About a year later the highway was officially opened allowing Squamish and Britannia citizens to drive into Vancouver and vice versa. As this highway now is extended to Whistler Ski Resort, it is referred to as the Sea to Sky Highway. We attended all these functions in our dress uniforms and provided traffic control and security. It is worthy of note that Whistler, B.C., did not exist at this particular time. However, it serves to graphically illustrate what development can take place when there are good transportation routes available. Many local business men had a dream of creating Whistler even in this era.

Emil Anderson Construction played a large role in the building of these two projects. One Monday morning after the rail line was open, the highway construction foreman reported that one of their large off-highway Euclid earthmovers had been totally destroyed by vandals. We attended the scene and found this enormous vehicle had been driven over a 150 to 200 foot cliff where it had landed on the railway tracks, bending both rails, then bounced into the ocean and eventually ended partially submerged in Howe Sound. This equipment and others had been parked at the job site for the week-end. We came to the conclusion that the person who committed this offence had to be knowledgeable in operating one of these machines. The foreman expressed his suspicions regarding a former employee who had been fired for various safety violations. We located this fellow and his girl friend in Squamish and interrogated them separately. The suspect denied any involvement, but his girl friend said he did it because he was mad about being fired and wanted to impress her. She stated he started the machine, drove it towards the cliff and jumped out. Since this incident she said she had been tempted to call the police several times because the act of vandalism had really bothered her. When this fellow was informed of his girl friend's statement, he entered a plea of guilty and was sent to Oakalla Prison Farm.

The Al Hendrickson Logging operation was about twenty miles south of Pemberton on the P.G.E. rail line at a siding especially installed for him called Hendrickson Siding. Hendrickson came to the office one day and reported that they had found what they believed to be a wartime Japanese balloon bomb and they were not too sure whether the explosives attached were still active or not. I took a freight train along with Hendrickson to the siding and we then hiked in about three miles to the location. Shreds of the paper balloon were still hanging from a large tree; the remainder of the balloon, including the incendiary devices, was lying on a large rock outcropping immediately below the tree. We counted six large incendiary bombs but there may have been others buried in the pine needles. Upon returning to Squamish, I made contact with the Canadian Army to obtain the services of a bomb disposal expert. Two days later an army sergeant arrived at Squamish and we returned to Hendrickson Siding and the site of the balloon bomb. The Sergeant confirmed that it was a Japanese bomb and it would appear all the bomb devices were active. He set small charges next to each one and using a long fuse detonated the incendiaries. I was amazed at the intensity of the fire from each one and watched them actually burn a hole in the rock where they were located. After they burned out we carefully searched the area for others but apparently there were no more. We did have an injury during this operation as the army sergeant, while returning to the railway tracks, stepped on a wasps' nest and was severely stung. Needless to say, the air was blue with profanity but unfortunately it had no effect on the wasps.

For the benefit of the readers who are not knowledgeable about the balloon bombs, I will give a short history of their origin. During World War II, the Japanese launched hundreds of these large hot air balloons from Japan. They were made from paper and would climb into the west to east jet stream with a purpose of starting forest fires on the North American west coast. Hanging from these balloons was a large metal ring. In this ring were shrouds hanging down with weights and incendiary bombs attached and as the balloon was travelling east from Japan it would begin to lose altitude. Explosive devices in the ring had barometric fuses set for certain altitudes and when fired, it would cut the shroud attached to one of the weights. Upon release of the weight the balloon would gain or maintain an altitude and this was so calculated that after all the weights had been used, the balloon would land in the North American forest and the incendiary devices would explode causing large forest fires. Since the war some have been found in Alaska, British Columbia, Washington and Oregon. I have heard of unconfirmed reports that one was found as far east as the Province of Manitoba.

It seems the stolen women's underwear caper kept following me around. The manager of the Woodfibre pulp mill called to report the theft of ladies' underwear from clothes- lines in the residential area, including that of his wife. He said he would send the tug-boat over and it would be at the Squamish dock in about one-half hour. I sent one of our junior constables who spent most of the afternoon investigating, and upon his return he briefed me on what he had ascertained. Apparently this was not the first incident at Woodfibre, but the first time for the manager's wife. It appears the ladies involved in the other incidents did not want to report the theft. I asked the constable if he could give me an idea if the women were attractive and about what age. He said they were very nice looking ladies and were quite old, about my age. Since I was thirty-three years old at the time, I told him I did not think I was old. This poor guy stuttered and stammered and was very embarrassed over his comment. We had no further complaints from Woodfibre, so we presumed its being such a close and isolated community, the thief elected to cease his activities particularly as the mill manager and the police had become involved.

While in Williams Lake I had a young hard-working constable, who was a good all-round investigator. He was selected by the Force to attend the University of British Columbia to study law. Before leaving, he married a local girl and they moved to Vancouver. We were all extremely shocked to learn the Vancouver City Police had arrested this man for exposing himself to young children near the university area. He was convicted and discharged from the Force. All who knew him could not bring themselves to think he would do such an act. We tried to search our minds to identify any previous incidents that would point to this type of activity at Williams Lake, but none could identify anything. While I was at the Vancouver Subdivision office, the superintendent summoned me to his office and proceeded to interrogate me about the young constable. The University of British Columbia came under R.C.M. Police Vancouver Subdivision jurisdiction, and therefore the Officer Commanding became involved as this member was attending that university. This officer would not let up in his questioning of me. He stated I must have known of his behaviour and why didn't I take appropriate action. When I told him nobody at Williams Lake detected any untoward behaviour by this member, he expressed total disbelief. The matter became very heated and I told him he could believe what he wanted but I was giving the true facts. That ended this discussion but I was so upset with this man I could hardly keep a civil tongue in my head. Nothing further came of this incident, but I was extremely disappointed by his overall attitude.

There was a bulletin published giving a description of a missing car and driver. Apparently an older couple from Ontario had hired this person, who was a neighbour, to drive them in their new car to British Columbia where they planned to visit relatives in the Cloverdale area near Vancouver. After arriving in B. C., the couple gave the driver the car to use while they were visiting but with the clear understanding that he would return to take them home on a certain date. He failed to appear. The elderly couple could not lay charges of theft as he had the car with their permission, after a long wait they flew back to Ontario. This is where the story takes a strange twist.

At Porteau the P.G.E. Railway and the highway between Squamish and North Vancouver run side by side a few feet above the ocean high tide for about a mile. A sheer cliff rises beside the road with Howe Sound on the other side of the railway. The railway section gang were working along this stretch and while sitting on the rocks by the ocean eating lunch, they spotted oil breaking on the surface some feet from shore. Attending the scene we verified that the oil was surfacing constantly. We obtained the services of our scuba divers and found a car about thirty feet under the surface. When it was pulled out of the water we identified it as the missing Ontario car. The key was in the ignition in the 'off' position, the car was in neutral, the emergency brake was off, no persons were found inside, the doors and the windows were shut, the left tail-light was broken and the left rear fender damaged. A search of the gravel shoulder of the road and the railway ballast revealed portions of the red glass we felt came from the tail-light of the car. At the same time curved skid marks on the blacktop were found leading to the tail-light lens. Our laboratory examined the found tail-light lens with the pieces removed from the car, and confirmed it as being a match. This evidence assisted us greatly in establishing that the car had been pushed by another vehicle over the tracks and into the ocean. What we were not able to establish was the reason for this incident or the whereabouts of the driver. Many months later we learned that he had been located in California so we asked that the elderly couple be interviewed and lay a charge of wilful damage should he return to Canada. They declined and that is the last we heard of the matter. We speculate that this person took this unique opportunity to pull off a disappearing act. We were able to establish there was a second person involved who brought along the other vehicle to push the missing vehicle into the ocean. I guess you could say we didn't get our man, but we had found him.

As previously mentioned, Pacific Great Eastern Railway (now B.C. Rail) was our main source of transportation, particularly between Squamish and Seton Portage. In one case the locals at Alta Lake advised us that they had not seen a long-time resident of their area for some time and were concerned as to his welfare. He resided in the woods off the track between Alta Lake and Garibaldi. We established the railway milepost; then two members were dispatched to investigate. They boarded a freight train at the North Yards, and when the train got to the milepost, the engineer stopped the caboose and our two members got off. The dispatcher then alerted the southbound freights with instructions to stop and pick the men up when seen on the side of the track. The two constables found the missing person dead at his residence, placed him in a body bag, sealed up his cabin and carried him to the track side to wait for the next southbound freight. Upon its arrival again the engineer would put the caboose at their disposal. The body was hoisted onto the rear vestibule of the caboose and taken to Squamish. The old fellow had died of natural causes.

Another particular instance of our reliance on the P.G.E. involved a bootlegger who lived between D'Arcy and Mount Currie. He was selling liquor to the Indians on Mount Currie Indian Reserve although at this time Indians were not permitted to have liquor on their reserves. Several attempts to raid his place had failed, as each time he was notified in advance of our arrival. This time two of us boarded a passenger train out of Squamish and rode in the baggage car with Conductor Harry Lassman and two others. Our member there was instructed to wait for fifteen minutes after our departure, then drive for the suspect's residence by police vehicle, which would take him through the Mount Currie Reserve. By this time we would be very close to the residence which was about eight to ten miles north of the reserve and very close to the road and the railway. It was 10 p.m. when the train stopped opposite his residence and we got off. When he answered our knock at the door he had a surprised look on his face. We served him with a copy of the Search Warrant, and a very short while later the member from Pemberton arrived to assist. We found that he was in liquor manufacturing in a big way. We took samples, then dumped gallons of material from large containers and broke them up. He was arrested and all four of us returned to Pemberton where he was locked up. Then two of us returned to Squamish by freight in the wee small hours of the morning. This is how the railway assisted us to short circuit the information which alerted this bootlegger of our arrival each time we drove through the   reserve.

The foregoing two stories are examples of the many instances where the Pacific Great Eastern Railway assisted the police in transporting them into difficult and out of the way points where no other transport was available. I cannot offer enough praise to the railway management, dispatchers, engineers, firemen, conductors, trainmen and agents for their continued assistance and co-operation at all times. At this particular period, the railway was very busy and was becoming more so every year, but it never did lose its friendly family attitude and I sincerely hope it never does.

In the early part of our posting to Squamish, Brittania Mine was still operating. It was reputed to have twenty-two miles of tunnel, much of it under Howe Sound. On one occasion there had been a fatality underground at the mine which I attended. This was my one and only underground experience, and I quickly came to the conclusion that mining was not for me. We travelled for what seemed a very long time to get to the accident site and our return seemed even longer. Miners have my healthy respect for working in the mines day after day for years on end with the constant dangers that are inherent in the occupation.

For example, B.C. Hydro was constructing a dam at Garibaldi on the Cheakumas River, and punching a hole through the mountain for five miles to come out over the Mamquam River where they installed penstocks to a power house under construction. The tunnelling was being done from both ends. The crew at the Garibaldi end had an accident where a person was killed as a result of a rock fall. Investigation revealed the person's name was Tallarico and he was the shift boss. They had just fired a round (blasted) and it was his duty to go in and check the ceiling and walls at the blast site for possible rock falls. He had just gone forward when a large slab came down on him. A friend of mine by the name of George Reed, who was also a member of the Force, called me from Bowen Island to advise the deceased person was his wife's uncle. As we had no road or rail as yet, George came to Squamish by water taxi to recover the body for burial in Trail, B.C. This particular incident reinforced my attitude about working underground.

The highlight of our Squamish posting came in January, 1959, when we were informed that our long awaited baby boy, who was one month old, was about to join our little family, a truly great joy to Margaret, me, and Patti, who was now five years old. We named our new son Bruce Allan, a good Scottish name according to Margaret's mother, who had emigrated from Scotland.

That same year Patti started grade one at the Mashiter Elementary School, the same school where Margaret had spent her primary years in earlier times.

One day I received a phone call from the superintendent, requesting me to report to his office in Vancouver the next day at 10 a.m. My immediate thought was "What have I done now," considering all the perceived problems he had over a missing fifty cent piece and other matters. At the meeting he advised me that he was having difficulty with the management of the detachment at the Provincial Court House in downtown Vancouver, referred to as Vancouver Town Station. He said he was going to remove the staff sergeant in charge and the sergeant was retiring to pension. He wanted me to move to Vancouver and take the Sergeant's position. What could I say? This is the first time I had ever been asked if I wanted a transfer and also a promotion, so I immediately agreed. This was early in December, 1959, and later that month I received a memo that I was to report to Vancouver Town Station on December 23rd. I sent a memo back advising that I was not moving my family on Christmas Eve but I would move in January. The boss acknowledged and gave his approval. As a departing gift we were presented with a television set at a farewell party hosted by the Squamish business community and friends. It was an overwhelming gift as Squamish had no television signals at that time, but our move to Vancouver, of course, changed all that.

33. Premier W.A.C. Bennett of British Columbia, (centre) and cabinet ministers at the opening of the P.G.E. Railway extension from Squamish to North Vancouver, B.C., 1958.

34. Attorney General Robert Bonner (left) chatting with the author at the opening of the railway extension.

35. Squamish Detachment building with office on the left and living quarters on the right.

36. Powerful Vancouver tug boat *Sudbury* at Squamish harbour docking rail barges. This vessel earned great notoriety for its mid-Pacific salvage rescues of freighters in distress.

Chapter 12

Vancouver Town Station Detachment

1960 to 1963

Our move to Vancouver was a major adjustment for both of us, as we would be living in the suburbs and I would commute to the centre of the city for work. My replacement in Squamish was a Corporal Henry Routledge who was being moved off Vancouver Drug Squad and back into uniform. We rented his house in the Dunbar area of the city; we sort of traded houses. This fellow was no relation to me, and from the comments of Squamish residents he had a very different and difficult personality. The fact that we had the same name caused some problems with the administration which didn't sit well with me. Even our bank was confused. It was not the most brilliantly conceived transfer. To make a long story short, Henry Routledge spent three years in Squamish and then was sent to Drug Squad in Toronto where he was eventually disciplined and discharged from the Force.

At Vancouver Town Station, the staff sergeant who was to be transferred took his pension instead and was replaced by Staff Sergeant Tom Kelly. The sergeant whom I was to replace retired also. This is one time I had to agree with the superintendent: Tom Kelly and I had accepted a can of worms. Our stenographer was the wife of the staff sergeant who had just retired, and during their tenure she seemed to have run the detachment. This was an unhealthy situation, as she felt she had inherited her husband's authority. Tom Kelly put her in her place very quickly by making her office out of bounds to all personnel and herself answerable only to Kelly or me. Later Tom had the unenviable task of taking her aside and telling her to clean her clothes. She wore the same dress everyday for months, it was filthy, and he also suggested she take a shower or a bath to look after her personal hygiene. As a result, she retired a short while later.

Not too long after our arrival at Vancouver, I received some distressing news. Staff Sergeant Stan Rothwell, Special Constable Ray Cormier and a Constable Green were conducting an air search along hills beside Skaha Lake near Penticton for a kidnap suspect when the Beaver aircraft was caught in a down draft and struck one of the hills. The crash killed all on board. Stan's wife Helen asked if I would be one of the pallbearers. Needless to say, this accident was a great loss for the Force and very upsetting to me. Stan was a gentleman, a friend and an excellent pilot, as his many thousands of flying hours will attest. A cairn in Penticton commemorates the loss of these three members.

Duties of the members of Vancouver Town Station were to meet with a prison van all planes, trains, busses and boats from other parts of British Columbia and take the escorts and their prisoners to the various institutions. We were also responsible for bringing in prisoners from the Provincial Gaol to our office and then escorting them from the cells to the various supreme courts in the building. We would stay as guards in court during deliberations and then return them to Oakalla Prison Farm at the end of the day.

Personnel consisted of roughly ten young members recently out of training in Regina, and the other five or so consisted of constables with ten or more years who had been stationed elsewhere, failed in whatever they were to do and eventually ended up here as a last resort. Their attitude, work ethic, and uniform dress habits certainly demanded constant monitoring and correction. They were really dead wood but unfortunately no action could be taken unless there was a flagrant breach of regulations; these senior constables knew where to draw the line to avoid being discharged as unsuitable. With constant prodding by two corporals and me, supported by S/Sgt. Kelly, we eventually got a little more active mileage out of these people. The younger constables just out of training were terrific, as they were anxious to prove themselves. They wanted their tenure at Vancouver Town Station to be over with and then be posted to a detachment for some real police work.

Over the years I watched their progress and the majority did very well.

One of the senior constables was McNeil, a practical joker who had one speed: dead slow. Members guarding prisoners in the supreme courts, such as Assize, B. C. Appeal Courts or County Court were required to wear red serge uniforms. When the courts adjourned for a break, they would bring their prisoners back to the cells and have a coffee break.McNeil enjoyed pulling tricks on the younger members but some went beyond a joke. One of McNeil's favourites was stirring his hot coffee with a metal spoon, watching until one of the new constables put his coffee to his lips. Then McNeil would touch his victim's cup hand with the hot spoon. The immediate reaction was a jerk of the arm, which ended with the young fellow spilling hot coffee down the front of his red serge uniform. The member, of course would not have time to change into another uniform and, besides, it required the expense of cleaning. I had heard that this was one of McNeil's tricks and I hoped I would be present when he did it. One day I got my wish. McNeil laughed and looked at me to see if I saw the humour. I immediately reprimanded him for being so damned stupid and advised him he would pay the cleaning bill or I would have him charged under our disciplinary code. The younger members really enjoyed seeing McNeil stutter while trying to make logic out of this act. We never again had this problem.

Some of these young men, of course, were out for revenge. While McNeil's stetson hat was hanging on the rack, one young constable broke a wooden pencil in half, cut a straight pin, inserted one end into the broken end of the pencil and pushed it through the brim of the hat and into the other half of the pencil. As a result the lead pencil looked as if it had been pushed right through the brim. S/Sgt. Tom Kelly and I were in his office talking when all of a sudden McNeil rushed in waving his stetson around and complaining about what those kids had done to it. While he was trying to explain the situation, one half of the pencil fell onto Tom's desk, followed by the other half. McNeil stopped shouting. We both stared at him and Tom asked him what the problem was while examining the brim of the stetson. All that appeared was a very tiny pin hole. Tom told McNeil to stop complaining about trivial matters and get back to work. I told the younger fellows later as to what had happened in the office and they all had a good laugh over McNeil's discomfiture.

Three years for me at this place was enough. Both Tom Kelly and I agreed, however, there was marked improvement in the members of the whole detachment from appearance to attitude. Our observations were supported by the superintendent. I was selected for transfer to Grand Forks, British Columbia, in 1964.

Chapter 13

Grand Forks Detachment

1964 to 1965

My move was precipitated by the present N.C.O. in charge of the detachment who apparently had committed some breach of discipline. The community was quite aware of the situation and became upset by this turn of events. He was transferred immediately.

We rented a house owned by a Japanese Canadian potato farmer named Sigumoto. 'Siggy,' as we knew him, and his wife Fran were wonderful landlords and we became good friends. Grand Forks had a population of approximately 3,000, about sixty percent of whom were Orthodox Doukhobor and forty percent of other ethnic origins. The same ratio applied to the business community. The area was very laid back and had a low crime rate. The southern boundary of the city was less than a mile from the U.S border. One border crossing was located immediately west of the city off Highway 3 and the other, just south of Christina Lake. Highway 3 is the southern trans-provincial highway running through the centre of the city. The first community to the west was the famous old mining and smelting community of Greenwood and to the east after Christina Lake was Castlegar, reached by travelling over the Blueberry-Paulson Pass. The Detachment consisted of eight members, two of whom were on Highway Patrol. They covered from Christian Valley-Rock Creek through to the top of the Blueberry-Paulson Pass.

The detachment needed a little housecleaning. It appeared that nobody was in charge, each member doing his own thing; consequently, there appeared to be confusion and lack of purpose. One small matter was the fact that several members were frequenting the beer parlours of the local hotels during their off duty hours. I had a policy that members did not fraternize in the local drinking establishments, as this practice could lead to a conflict of interest. I was fully supported by most of the members. Over a short period of time we had arrested several intoxicated persons found leaving the hotel beer parlours. All indications were that contrary to the Liquor Control Act they had been served while already intoxicated. One day I took the members who had been frequenting these establishments and met with the owner-operators, advising them that serving a person until he was intoxicated, or when intoxicated, would not be tolerated. A continuance of these offences could lead to charges being laid and the possible suspension of their liquor licence by the B.C. Liquor Control Board for at least two weeks. After the meeting the younger members very well understood the reason for my policy. Thus ended the problems with the members and the hotels during the remainder of my stay - with one later exception.

Each day the Highway Patrol would set out to various locations, always the same day of the week. When they went to Rock Creek every Tuesday, they would go up the Christian Valley and check logging trucks for over length and over height, plus proper insurance and licences. The next day I would inquire how the trip had gone and their standard response was very good; all the logging trucks were complying. Despite their protests I instructed them to rotate the days in these areas. The following week they were in Christian Valley they stopped at least four logging trucks for non-compliance. The logging truck operators soon found Tuesday was not always Highway Patrol day.

Corporal Frank Leitkeman was the man in charge of Greenwood Detachment and was quite a character. As he often pulled little jokes on us, I thought there had to be a day of retribution. I found one. The Canadian Audubon Society had somehow got the ear of our Commissioner in Ottawa, who instructed us to make monthly reports on the number of bald eagle sightings in our detachment areas. This task was an absolute pain which created more paper work; however, if you had no sightings for three months you were not required to put in any further reports. Consequently, Greenwood and

Grand Forks and many other detachments had no reports. I had been to Greenwood visiting Frank, and on my way home I sighted a bald eagle on a tree near the highway just east of his town. When I got back, I submitted a report to the commissioner of my sighting, and a copy to Frank noting that Greenwood would be sending in monthly reports from here on. There was a phone call from Frank with a lot of cursing and then some good laughs and threats of retaliation.

The brand inspector for the provincial government came to the office one day and reported that a person had been selling and shipping unbranded cattle. He had all the documentation and witnesses. We interviewed and took statements from the witnesses and then applied for a warrant to arrest. The person we wanted was the same one who had caused the problem with my predecessor and brought about his removal from Grand Forks. The suspect lived north-west of Grand Forks on a bench of land that overlooked the city and the valley. The route to his place was a switchback road up the side hill and then about a quarter mile to his house, which fortunately was out in the open. The plan was for me wearing civilian clothes and using my own car to drive up to his house followed by others in police cars, who would stop on the hill just below out of sight. When I lit a cigarette they would come to the house at top speed. The plan worked. When I saw him approaching, I lit the cigarette and offered him one. He had his back to the road and by the time he realized what was going on, I had placed him under arrest and had the handcuffs on him. The entire matter was over within a few minutes. This fellow had a bad reputation so we were glad to get him in the cells without incident. He was convicted of the charge and fined.

The provincial Liquor Act stated that continued abuses of alcohol could result in the person's appearance before a magistrate and his being declared an interdict. This is an over-simplification of the wording in the Liquor Act, but the ramifications eventually led to a serious shooting offence. In Grand Forks a person named Remezoff had, prior to my time, been declared an interdicted person. He was not allowed to enter any licenced premises, liquor stores, or be in possession of liquor at any time, and any person who supplied him with liquor was subject to a similarly heavy penalty and immediate arrest.

Constable Geisbecht and Robinson were on foot patrol in the city one late evening when they saw Remezoff getting into his car with what appeared to be a bottle of liquor in his hand. The members pursued him to his residence located in the southwest corner of the city, but by the time they arrived, Remezoff had entered the house. After they had knocked on the door several times, it suddenly flew open and Remezoff came out with a rifle in his hand. The two members immediately ran for cover behind the police car and four shots were fired into the vehicle. Remezoff then went in and closed the door. Both members retreated on foot to an Irrigation Sales and Service building where the owner happened to be in his office doing his books. He gave Robinson a ride to the detachment and fortunately every member was present, as the local auxiliaries were attending a weekly class. After being briefed on the situation, we took the gas gun and rifle from the locker and proceeded to the area. The auxiliaries were instructed to stay at the office and attend the phone and radio. After positioning members around the house in the dark, I took the gas gun and entered the property from the rear into the garden, where I could barely distinguish an outline of the house. I took a shot at a small window in the rear of the house with the gas gun, but missed and hit the window frame. My second shot went through the window into the house. We heard the back door open and then dead silence, so we presumed he was outside, but it was so dark we could not see. A rifle shot rang out and then there was silence. I heard a noise very close to where I was lying on the ground and could see a silhouette of a person standing about ten feet away. I fired a shot from my revolver at the silhouette, which was answered by another rifle shot. Immediately a spotlight from the Irrigation Office window shone into the garden. The voice of the owner said Remezoff was lying in the garden and was not moving, so I crawled forward and found him lying face down in the dirt.

He had a bullet wound to the lower jaw and was bleeding badly. A quick roll call ensured all members were well. Remezoff was taken to the hospital and placed under guard.

We then had a debriefing at the scene. Constables Geisbecht and Robinson related what had happened from their perspective, and we found the gas round that had missed the target. Constable Lowe had been at the back of the house at the opposite corner of the garden to mine next to an old shed, and had used it and a cedar fence post as cover. The shot that Remezoff fired while on the back porch was at Constable Lowe. The bullet had hit the fence post just inches above his head and showered him with splinters of cedar. The second gas shell I fired into the house did work, as the house smelled of the gas which probably had driven him out into the back yard. The police car was badly damaged with bullet holes in one side and out the other. One had penetrated the motor. Later examinations showed metal splinters had entered the motor requiring a new motor exchange. The owner of the Irrigation Company was delighted with the outcome and said he would be ready to testify if and when required. He took a great risk in showing the spotlight, as we had no idea what Remezoff was going to do next. This man certainly received our heartfelt thanks for the assistance he rendered.

At the hospital I found Remezoff was out of emergency and in a ward. He was later taken to the larger hospital at Trail. Doctor Perley said he had only one bullet wound and that was to the jaw, and in his view the only way it could have been inflicted was by Remezoff himself with a rifle. It appears he intended to commit suicide by putting the rifle under his chin but instead blew away part of his left jaw. The lack of another wound indicates to me that my revolver shot had missed him.

I contacted my Officer Commanding, Superintendent John Stevenson in Nelson, and apprised him of the events as they had occurred. He said he would be right over, which meant in about one and a half to two hours. Since by this time it was 2 a.m., so all members not involved in the guarding were allowed to go home, as I did also for a few hours before returning to the office at 4:30 a.m. when I learned that the ambulance had left for Trail with the prisoner. I met with the Officer Commanding and gave him a complete briefing to which he expressed how pleased he was that none of the members were injured and the offender was in custody. The Section N.C.O. from Nelson was with him. His view was that I should not have taken direct action but rather contacted him personally and waited for his assistance. I said; "What you wanted me to do was call out to Mr. Remezoff and advise him to wait for several hours until help arrived from ninety miles away and then we would resume the shooting match." I further said that under the given circumstances what he was suggesting was absolutely ridiculous. Action had to be taken immediately in order to bring this man under control. Superintendent Stevenson with a smile on his face concurred completely with the action I had taken.

Several months later, Supt. Stevenson called and advised that the commissioner had awarded a Commendation for Bravery to Constable Lowe, Constable Geisbrecht and me. This news came as a complete surprise to all three of us, as the R.C.M.Police is not known to readily hand out commendations. Obviously, the superintendent had recommended us for the awards. Remezoff was convicted in the Kamloops Assize Court and sentenced to nine years in the penitentiary. Several years later, Supt. Stevenson called me to advise that Remezoff had died there from cancer.

It was interesting to learn many months later that the R.C.M.Police had written to the Crown Prosecutor advising him confidentially that we were being considered for commendations. However, before these were awarded, they wanted the Prosecutor to confirm that our testimonies were exactly the same as in the reports I had submitted. After the trial the Prosecutor wrote a response stating that the testimony of all the participants was as reported and in some instances more elaborate. He further stated that he personally was amazed and impressed at the cool and calm approach of the members of the force during such a highly volatile situation.

In the R.C.M.Police, when a member qualified at the compulsory annual target practice on the revolver range, he received a crossed-revolvers badge to be sewn on the sleeve of his jacket; the same applied in rifle shooting, where he received a crossed-rifles badge. Over the years I had failed to reach the required points to qualify. Several weeks after the Remezoff incident an envelope arrived from Trail Detachment and inside was a replica of our crossed-revolvers badge, only the revolvers had been replaced with miniature, crossed fly swatters. Staff Sergeant Beaumont, who was in charge of the Trail Detachment, was a humorous character and this was his way of telling me I did not qualify for crossed revolvers, only for crossed fly swatters. My marksmanship certainly supported his conclusions.

One member of the detachment caused me concern. He was lazy, he could not be relied upon and he was tardy in investigations and other files. He had separated from his wife, she had returned to her parents, and he had begun frequenting the beer parlours again. I asked for his transfer from Grand Forks, and the Officer Commanding agreed and he was sent to Nelson, residing as a single member in barracks. Our paths would cross again within months.

Another member of my detachment was under internal investigation because of some matter that had occurred at the last detachment where he was stationed. The investigators came to Grand Forks several times and interviewed him. I was then advised by my Officer Commanding that he had just received word that this constable was to be charged with breaches of the R.C.M.Police disciplinary code. I so informed him and I left on annual leave. Upon my return I learned that he had attempted suicide in the basement of his home using his service revolver. He blew away a fair portion of his brain but somehow survived. He was later discharged from the Force.

Chapter 14

Special 'D' Section, Nelson, B.C.

1965 to 1966

At the turn of the century Russian immigrants, referred to as Doukhobors, came to Canada to avoid persecution by the Czar. They settled in Saskatchewan for a few years and then a large number moved to southern British Columbia in areas around Castlegar, Krestova, Grand Forks and Nelson. Webster's Dictionary refers to a Doukhobor as "a member of a Christian Sect of 18th century Russian origin emphasizing the duty of obeying the inner light and rejecting church or civil authority." The majority of this sect assimilated into the Canadian way of life by becoming successful farmers and business people. A breakaway group, however, referred to themselves as the Sons of Freedom or Svobodniki, and absolutely rejected the Doukhobor doctrine and all civil law. They would set fire to their own homes and disrobe to watch them burn. They paraded down the streets of Nelson, Castlegar and Grand Forks in the nude to symbolise that they had divested themselves of any worldly goods. Because they refused to send their children to school, the provincial government set up a separate school for them at New Denver; the children were rounded up and taken to this school where they had to remain. The parents were given visiting privileges only. Their disregard for the laws and criminal acts of violence against other persons' property were extremely difficult to investigate as the Sons of Freedom were a close-knit group.

Over the years their activities became extremely serious, causing deaths and near-death in several incidents. The C.P.R., B.C.Hydro, and other facilities were attacked with bombs many times. The Svobodniki were, without a doubt, terrorists creating criminal acts against the citizens of Canada. They put a torch to several fruit-packing warehouses in the Okanagan Valley, causing lay-offs of many workers.

Bombing of the C.P.R. tracks and trestles could have caused serious injury or death to the train crews. In one incident these extremists came close to creating the largest murder case in Canadian history. B.C. Hydro has a high voltage line suspended nearly a mile across Kootenay Lake near the mining community of Riondel. These power lines were suspended hundreds of feet above the water from enormous towers built onto the mountainsides, and the power from them supplied many communities including Riondel and the mine. The tower on the west side of the lake was bombed causing it to collapse, and sending the power lines into the water. All power was immediately cut off to the mine. The mine shaft went well below and under Kootenay Lake, and the sudden lack of power brought the large pumps to a stop. Immediately the mine shaft started to fill with water, and the fifty or so miners underground were forced to run for their lives only minutes before the flood. The police had a difficult time preventing these miners from taking vigilante action against the Sons of Freedom Doukhobors, as they immediately became prime suspects.

Another incident had a serious effect on the Sons of Freedom themselves. During one of their ventures into the Okanagan where we believe they were going to attack a fruit-packing plant, the bomb device exploded prematurely in the car killing both occupants.

Although the Sons of Freedom were supposed to be practising what their religion told them, that is, not to follow man's law or any Christian belief, they soon learned they needed licence plates for their vehicles, and drivers' licences for themselves as required by the British Columbia Motor Vehicles Act. They also learned quickly that in order to get any welfare or other government hand-outs, they were required to apply under the appropriate government legislation, and they did. These people were very hypocritical.

Rather than having each detachment in the Kootenays and the Okanagan investigating the bombing and burning incidents, the R.C.M.Police formed a group of investigators to concentrate solely on apprehending the offenders. This group was named Special 'D' Section and consisted of a member in charge and seven other men, some of whom spoke Russian. The Special 'D' Section was commanded by Staff Sergeant John Stinson, an excellent investigator and a very fine man. During all this lengthy turmoil, John showed indications that he needed rest and he was taken off this duty and replaced. It came as a great shock when, after only one year in Grand Forks, I was selected to replace him. This appointment of course meant a transfer to Nelson and the usual upheaval of the family; however, the prospects of a promotion to staff sergeant lessened the agony of yet another move within a year.

After many years of investigation, Staff Sergeant Stinson and his Section had had a great deal of success, apprehending over 130 people who were charged, convicted and sentenced to lengthy prison terms. A special prison called Mountain Prison was built at Agassiz in the Fraser Valley where they were incarcerated. The remaining members, about 600, then staged a march from the Kootenays to Agassiz, a distance of well over 300 miles, where they set up a cardboard box shack town outside the prison, which remained for years.

The Special 'D' Section operated out of the Nelson Sub- division Headquarters in Nelson. The Section had been split, with one man now stationed in Chilliwack monitoring the Sons of Freedom who were camped outside the prison gates at Agassiz. Their illegal activities in the Kootenays suddenly ceased, and we deduced the right ones were in gaol. The prison was built to be as fireproof as possible, but these rebellious prisoners still managed to set fire to the mattresses as a show of protest against man's law.

The National Parole Board began to set hearings in Chilliwack for some of the prisoners. I was selected by the Attorney General of B.C. to represent his office at these hearings and to give the police perspective on each individual. The Attorney General wrote stating that whatever view I gave, he fully supported. At the same time we had full support from the Officer Commanding Chilliwack Subdivision, Inspector E.W. Willes and his staff. As time went on the frequency of hearings increased and I spent much of my time in Chilliwack. Participating at these parole hearings was interesting. Each individual would be dealt with separately. The Prison Warden would address the Board, followed by the Parole Officer and the police representing the Attorney General, all having input on each of these prisoners. Ironically, in many instances, we would be advocating certain individuals be released on parole while the prison and parole officers would argue to the contrary. The stance taken in many cases by the police came about because we knew more about these prisoners than the others as a result of our many years of investigation. We knew who were the least dangerous and those who were the ring leaders. In most cases our input was accepted and the lesser lights were released on parole. We would then tell them that we as police had confidence in their proper behaviour and trusted them not to let us down. We had no problem with these individuals thereafter.

As much of our squad activity was now in the Chilliwack area, I arranged to have Sgt. Peever and two members transferred to that point. This plan worked out well, as they were able to monitor the Doukhobors' activities constantly as the prisoners would go to the shack town outside the gates when they were released. It was also interesting to watch the disintegration of this group, although slowly, taking place over the years both in the Kootenays and in the Chilliwack area. The trouble-makers were still in prison and the others felt a sense of relief from the Doukhobor doctrine and were able to get on with life. This was particularly noticeable in the younger generation, as they drifted away from the families in both areas and sought work in Vancouver and other parts of Canada. Some sought higher education and successful careers. Over the decades there has been the odd flare-up of activity, such as, setting minor fires, nude parades and starvation protests, but the participants became noticeably fewer, and this trend has continued to where there are no incidents for years on end.

I worked under Superintendent John Stevenson, a fine man who had served in Italy with the Canadian Army during the war and had worked his way up through the ranks. He understood the problems in police work and gave full support when he deemed it necessary. He also would not stand for any activities that would bring about embarrassment to the Force. I mentioned earlier on about a member in Grand Forks who was a problem in the detachment and eventually was moved to Nelson and resided in barracks. Well, it seems this young fellow was destined for trouble wherever he was stationed. I had a Russian-speaking single member, Constable Huska, also living in barracks at Nelson Subdivision, advise me he saw this chap and another person who happened to be a member of the Nelson City Police go by his door one evening, each carrying a set of skis. He thought it strange as Robinson was always broke and could ill afford to buy skis. Before talking to me, Huska had gone to the Nelson City Police and checked to see if any skis had been reported missing. Sure enough, a report had been filed of two sets stolen off the roof racks of a car parked in a residential area. I reported this matter to Superintendent Stevenson who had his Section N.C.O. investigate, and the skis were found behind the door of this member's room. He and the constable from the Nelson City Police were charged with theft and the young constable had his R.C.M.P. career come to an abrupt end.

Superintendent Stevenson was away on leave when the telephone rang in my office one day. It was Assistant Commissioner Spalding, the Commanding Officer for British Columbia in Victoria, telling me that he had just received a call from the Commissioner in Ottawa advising him that I had been promoted to the commissioned rank of Sub-Inspector. Later I was told my new duties were that of Criminal Intelligence Liaison Officer for Western Canada and I would be moved to Vancouver. Margaret and I were ecstatic about the promotion, the new job and moving back to Vancouver.

Chapter 15

Criminal Intelligence Liaison Officer

Western Canada

1966 to 1972

Two Criminal Intelligence Liaison Officers, one for Western Canada and one for Eastern Canada were newly-created positions within the R.C.M.Police. I was selected to the Western Canadian position and Inspector Maurice Nadon was selected for the eastern position working out of Montreal. The creation of these duties was brought about by the lack of co-operation between police forces throughout Canada and the U.S.A., a problem that was playing entirely into the hands of organized crime, who were definitely organized while the police were not. In 1966 at an annual meeting of the Canadian Association of Chiefs of Police, it was unanimously agreed to have these two positions created, and full co-operation was promised in reducing the jealousies and animosity that presently prevailed.

We were transferred to Vancouver and managed to find a house to rent in Burnaby. My office was to be in the Vancouver Subdivision building at 33rd and Heather Streets. However I was not destined to start the job right away as there was a slight change in the plans. As the Officer Commanding Burnaby Detachment was retiring and his replacement from Ottawa was not due to arrive for three months, I was selected as the interim boss of Burnaby, a detachment of 120 members at that time. This was a busy place but time seemed to drag as I was anxious to get on with the new duties for which I had been appointed. Eventually I took over my new function in September, 1967. As this was an entirely new position, with no precedent or policy to follow, I had to create my own plan and approach to the large scope of my duties. I commenced five years of constant travel, since my territory also included the northern U.S. from Minneapolis to Seattle and Portland, Oregon, and was eventually extended south into Los Angeles, San Francisco, Oakland, Sacramento, Salt Lake City and Denver, to name a few.

I visited the chiefs of every major police force in western Canada plus the northern U.S. and on our own commanding officers and criminal investigation officers of each division (province). I also spent long periods of time with the newly created Criminal Intelligence Units in each major populated area. I was well received by the chiefs of police and the majority of our senior officers, but of course we always seemed to have a few who were stumbling blocks in any new plan. One commanding officer felt that our Force was superior and he didn't need the likes of me to overcome the animosity that existed at that time between him and the local police chief. He failed to see that the friction caused by his attitude had to be overcome at the working level in order to accomplish our goal. Fortunately, I was fully supported by the Director of Criminal Investigations and the Deputy Commissioner of Operations in Ottawa who monitored my progress very closely. I did not ever have to call on either of them to intervene, as I was eventually able to convince the doubters of the logic of the new approach.

Over the first two years, the co-operation generated among all police forces was overwhelming. Joint investigations were started with each and every person assigned to criminal intelligence participating to the fullest. All major police forces made space available in their buildings and R.C.M.P. members were assigned on an equal man for man basis with the municipal force. In many instances we moved to a separate building, such as, Criminal Law Enforcement Unit in Vancouver (C.L.E.U.), where none of our investigations would be jeopardized by inquisitive, unauthorized persons. There were instances where attempts were made, and of course the investigators immediately became suspicious of these individuals and their ulterior motives.

The position I occupied was originally in Vancouver, but my constant and lengthy travelling prompted my move to Edmonton, more central to the western Canadian scene and a good location. I was provided with an office in 'K' Division H.Q. and a car, which gave me all the necessary requirements. Not too long after this move, my boss, the Director of Criminal Investigation (D.C.I.) in Ottawa, advised that my territory was to include eastern Canada as well. Inspector Nadon had been promoted and moved to another duty and I was to cover his area until his replacement was appointed.

There was one example of superb co-operation between one municipal police force and our Force which was greatly assisted by the chief of police, one officer from their C.I.D. and three plain-clothes members. The R.C.M. Police supplied an equal number of men. The joint operation had been gathering intelligence on a group who were robbing banks throughout the prairie provinces and other provinces. They were heard over wire taps planning to rob a bank in a city on a certain date and time. The Criminal intelligence units set up a joint surveillance and were prepared to intervene. While they waited, the telephone tap revealed a call to the robbers advising them of the police trap waiting for them. As a result they didn't attempt the robbery and the whole plan fell apart. The Criminal Intelligence group immediately started to analyze their situation to determine the source of the leak. They decided it had to be one of their own. Three of the members identified the voice on the phone as one of their men. Needless to say the concern was genuine; now they must decide if they would go to their chief or report to the Commanding Officer of R.C.M.P. They chose the Commanding Officer, and his assistant and at the same time asked that I be advised.

I was summoned from Edmonton and immediately briefed. After considerable discussion I suggested that I meet with chief and apprise him of the situation to date and see what action he would take, as I was from out of town and would not ruffle too many feathers. I had also known chief when he was a member of the R.C.M.P. and had other meetings with him as Chief of Police during the formation of the Criminal Intelligence group. I met with him at 2 p.m. that day and took copies of the wire tap transcript with me. Shocked and surprised, he advised he would attend to this matter and he thanked me for bringing this difficult situation to his attention. I returned to Edmonton. The next day I was phoned and advised that chief had taken immediate action. Confronted with the evidence, the officer admitted his guilt and was suspended immediately. While waiting for disciplinary action he decided to terminate his police service and departed. The formation of joint Criminal Intelligence Units within police forces certainly cleaned up some existing unhealthy situations.

I made one trip through to Halifax, Nova Scotia; Charlottetown, Prince Edward Island; Fredricton and St.John, New Brunswick; including Montreal, Quebec City, Ottawa, Toronto, Hamilton, and Windsor. It became apparent that no one person could cover all this area and accomplish any degree of success. I worked at it for six months before an inspector in Montreal was appointed for the eastern area. I have to say that he was not a suitable appointment as he lacked an outgoing personality and demonstrated a lack of interest in and understanding of the duties. Fortunately, a short while later his shortcomings were identified by those in eastern Canada and he was transferred and replaced by Inspector Rodrique. This fellow was just the opposite to his predecessor and did a good job. For a while we travelled together, and when we would arrive at a hotel he would identify us as Routledge and Rodrique, a new dance team in town. The desk clerks all seemed to enjoy this humour.

After three years of constant travel, I spoke with my superior in Ottawa, the Director of Criminal Investigation, and requested that he might consider a transfer to duties with less travel and more conducive to a home life. Several months later I was transferred to routine in-house duties as Assistant Criminal Investigations Officer at 'K' Division

Headquarters, Edmonton. I had a five-day week with little or no travel and no transfer required. As a result the family and I acquired a trailer and roamed on holidays all over the country. Plus we were able to participate in all the social activities within the Force and with friends and the children were settled for five years in one province and in one school. The duties I was performing were nothing to write home about, so I will not elaborate. After two years I was transferred to Ottawa as the Officer in Charge of all criminal intelligence operations within the Force. This office had a second function: it was the Secretariat of National Crime Intelligence, the umbrella operation for all organized crime investigation in Canada, and it maintained the repository of information in Ottawa for use by qualified member police forces.

Chapter 16

Officer in Charge National Criminal Intelligence

Ottawa, Ontario

1972 to 1975

My transfer to Ottawa and these new duties appeared on the surface to be nothing more than paper pushing, but it flowered into a very interesting stage of my career. My promotion to superintendent made the pill of having to work in Headquarters, Ottawa, a little easier to swallow. The job was a busy one as I was wearing two hats. Staff Sergeant Kieth Deevy assisted me in getting the Secretariat organized which was my number one priority. Inspector Graham George took over the Criminal Intelligence Officer duties for Western Canada at Edmonton replacing Inspector Harry Nixon. Graham George was an excellent choice, as he had been with Criminal Intelligence at Ottawa since its inception. My second hat was being in charge of all the Criminal Intelligence operations in Canada for our Force. Later I helped to establish a member to the embassies in Bonn, Germany; London, England; Berne, Switzerland; Hong Kong; and Kingston, Jamaica. We had already established liaison personnel in Washington, D.C. and Rome, Italy. These offices dealt directly with the federal police agencies in the host countries concerning the movements of criminals and their activities that were of mutual interest. The results were excellent.

Graham George had developed Criminal Intelligence courses in Ottawa for all police forces conducting criminal intelligence operations and members of the Secretariat. These courses were well attended over the years. I presented lectures on the Ottawa, H.Q. operation. The Commissioner received requests from the International Association of Chiefs of Police in Washington, D.C. to have me lecture Canadian investigative technique. These lectures took me to

New York; Washington, D.C., Charlotte, North Carolina; Fort Lauderdale and Miami, Florida, to name a few.

Our Ottawa Headquarters included the Services Section which operated all of our necessary technical equipment and conducted research into new methods. We had received complaints from the field about the lack of the latest technical equipment, research and support from this Ottawa operation. The Technical Services was a separate entity under the command of an inspector and his second in command, a civilian. I suggested to my superior that this unit come under the umbrella of Criminal Intelligence for research, administration, personnel and budget, to which he agreed. Since that time this group has excelled in the technical field and has been of great assistance to the investigator in the field.

Surveillance was always a problem in policing, as there was no set pattern for training or continuity. Men were utilized from the various sections, such as, narcotics, liquor, criminal intelligence, homicide and others, as and when required. Surveillance requires team work, and if at all possible, total invisibility, but the present arrangements were unsatisfactory. I devised a plan and policy for the formation of special surveillance units in every major city in Canada, they were to be named the Special 'O' Section. Commissioner Nadon gave his approval and received the necessary funding from the Treasury Board. This new approach required a great deal of planning. I found a person in our Force, Inspector Howard Gillard, who had years of experience in surveillance within another part of our organization, and managed to have him seconded to Criminal Intelligence. He was placed in charge of organizing policy, personnel, training, accommodation, equipment and all the other necessary features. We made frequent trips to the field to talk to the commanding officers and others who had doubts as to the viability of such an operation. Howard Gillard did a tremendous job, as we were recruiting and operating training sessions in all cities within eight months and running full surveillance in just over a year. Special 'O'

Section was born. This group has more than justified its existence since its inception and I will say that many criminal operations have been successfully concluded by dedicated surveillance personnel. These people are available to any police investigation, not just in organized crime. The seriousness of the offence dictated the priority for their use, and a system of checks and balances was established.

My duties were many faceted. I was asked on occasion to attend meetings in Toronto with my counterpart in the Ontario Provincial Police, the Toronto Metro Police and their organization, called Criminal Intelligence Services Ontario. The Commanding Officer of the R.C.M.Police Ontario Division had the rank of chief superintendent and he was not too co-operative with the other police forces, my efforts or other joint police operations. Further, he did everything possible to keep me from attending joint meetings by ordering me to attend a meeting with him when I was scheduled to meet with the others. He would write stinging memos to the commissioner of our force advising that my efforts were undermining his command. Twice the commissioner and my supervisor, the Director of Criminal Investigation (D.C.I.), met with me on this matter and instructed me to carry on and to ignore the memos, as they would attend to the matter. I had no further complaints about my work from this Commanding Officer.

The Ottawa building trades included a union called the Lathers' Union, who were people who put up drywall and did the finishing in the interior of buildings. The local union boss in Ottawa was at odds with union head office in Hamilton. They wanted him out but he refused to resign. This conflict eventually led to acts of vandalism and arson on building projects being handled by the Ottawa union. One day while the local union boss was at work, a couple of thugs from Montreal arrived at his residence front door. When they were told by the teenage son his father wasn't home, they proceeded to beat this young fellow severely and told him to pass the message on to his dad. This whole situation had been brewing for months; this assault was the incident, along with acts of arson, which brought it to a head. The public demanded action, and in 1974 a Royal Commission of Inquiry into Certain Sectors of the Building Industry was called under Mr. Justice Harry Waisberg of the Ontario Supreme Court. I was asked to give testimony on the association of certain organized crime groups from Montreal, Daniel Gasbarrini of Hamilton and others. Our surveillance carried out over many months showed these people in meetings with their associates, which helped to tie the whole group together. I am in possession of Volume 1 of the Inquiry where my testimony is transcribed.

Several days after my testimony I received a letter from Gasbarrini in Hamilton in which he stated, "I was not in the Inquiry the other day, but from what I have been told, your testimony was absolute bull-shit and you are a lying son of a bitch. You have not heard the last of this matter." Shortly thereafter, the Criminal Intelligence Unit in Toronto advised me of unconfirmed information that a contract had been put out on my life. Although I did not take the threat too seriously, I advised Margaret to watch for any suspicious activity in the neighbourhood and not to open any parcels received. One day I came home from a trip to be shown an open gift mailed from her brother in Montreal. We again had a serious talk about opening parcels. In many ways Margaret shared the tensions of my work.

My mother-in-law, who had lived with us for five years while she struggled with breast cancer, died in Ottawa in October, 1973, at the age of 84 years.

In 1974 I fell ill with severe abdominal pain while in Victoria attending a meeting with the Attorney General of B.C. in company with Deputy Commissioner Ross. I was also scheduled to speak to the province of Alberta's Crown Attorneys' Conference in Jasper while on my way home. I flew from Victoria to Vancouver, borrowed a car and drove to Mission to visit my father who was in the hospital dying from cancer. He was under heavy sedation and did not know me. I then flew from Vancouver to Edmonton, attended the conference in Jasper, and flew home from Edmonton to Ottawa the next day.

When stationed in Ottawa, members of the Force were required to have any medical treatments conducted at the National Defence Medical College in Ottawa. I had been reporting to this group regularly for over a year about abdominal pains and they told me each time there was nothing wrong. I reported again on my return, they performed surgery immediately and found a malignant tumour obstructing the colon. Thanks to the lack of proper diagnosis a year earlier, I came very close to cashing in my chips. I submitted a report on the care received, as had others, and eventually the policy was changed. Members can now go to doctors of their choice. While in the hospital in Ottawa, my sister Kathleen called Margaret to advise that our father had died, age 82. I was unfortunately in no condition to attend the funeral.

Prior to this time when I came to the west coast on business, I would make a quick trip out to Mission to visit my father and his new wife. I detected during my visits that I was not too welcome. Our conversations were all centred on my brother Jim and his work at Kenworth Truck in Seattle, Washington. If it was late in the day I was never invited to remain for supper, so I would go downtown in Mission and eat in a cafe before heading back to Vancouver. For years I never did feel warm to my father but I somehow felt an obligation to visit him and check on his well being.

Inspector Nadon, my counterpart as Criminal Intelligence Liaison Officer for Eastern Canada, had over the years risen to become commissioner of the R.C.M.P. While talking to him one day, I mentioned I would like to return to western Canada. A few months later he advised me of my transfer to the position of Officer in Charge of the large Edmonton Subdivision, with the associated rank of Chief Superintendent. We were a little disappointed as we would have liked to have returned to British Columbia, but Edmonton was also like home to us.

To obtain promotions in the commissioned ranks, one was required to write a paper and present it to a board consisting of the commissioner, three deputy commissioners and a few lesser lights, pointing out a problem within the Force and suggesting a solution. I chose a controversial subject: "Corruption in the Force." I had researched examples in which members had committed offences, and the lack of proper investigation, or fraternization between the investigator and the accused had failed to bring a proper conclusion to these cases, much to the disappointment of other members and the general public. I had knowledge over the years of such cases, and others were supplied to me by friends. Needless to say, my paper raised a few eyebrows and I was given a bit of a rough time from one member of the board. In the end they all agreed that my presentation certainly indicated that something had to be done. Special investigation teams as I had suggested would be set up to respond whenever and wherever necessary in each Division, and selection of personnel was to be made carefully to avoid conflict of interest. I received my promotion. This internal investigation team mechanism is being utilized throughout the Force in Canada at the present time.

Chapter 17

Officer in Charge Edmonton Subdivision

Edmonton, Alberta

1975 to 1976

We moved from Ottawa to Edmonton in July, 1975, where I took charge of Edmonton Subdivision. I was immediately promoted to Chief Superintendent and commenced to discover what I had inherited. Edmonton Subdivision included over half the geography of Alberta. My jurisdiction ran from an east-west line from the B. C. border near Jasper east through Drayton Valley, Wetaskiwin, Camrose, to the Saskatchewan border including one half of Lloydminster. The entire territory comprised the northern section of the province to the North West Territories with the exception of the smaller Peace River Subdivision. My assistants were two uniformed inspectors who supervised the east and west sections respectively. In total, including civilian personnel, my command consisted of 720 people.

The economy of Alberta was booming in a great rush to drill for oil. Wells were seen wherever one travelled, and many were encountered on the highways being moved to new sites. The Town of Fort McMurray was exceptionally busy with Suncor constructing an oil processing plant in the northern tar sands. The town had a permanent population of about 6,000 persons and a transient work force population of 8,000. The camp at the Suncor site was so large, it had two cookhouses which fed 1,000 persons each at every sitting, and they both ran three sittings for each meal. I had occasions to eat in these cookhouses several times and found the organization flawless, as was the excellent calibre of the food. The company also provided a very large recreation hall and had received permission from the province for a liquor licence to operate a pub. The company would not permit gambling in the camp area and any misbehaviour meant immediate dismissal and an escort out of the camp gates.

Not surprisingly, our people had very little problem in the camp, but the same could not be said about the town of Fort McMurray eight miles away.

Fort McMurray Detachment was having morale problems, partly because of the heavy work-load and partly because of the undercurrent created by one corporal and poor management by the staff sergeant in charge. I interviewed one female constable who had been at this detachment for a year and a half and was on the point of resigning. She was well rated by her peers but said that she had absolutely no social life and could not and would not go anywhere in town because of the rough individuals that come with a boom town atmosphere. I asked if she would like a transfer and she was delighted. Upon my return to Edmonton the Staffing Branch moved her to Jasper. When I conducted an inspection of Jasper detachment about six months later, she advised she had no intentions of resigning as she was very happy and settled. When the staff sergeant in charge of Fort McMurray was advised of his transfer, he immediately resigned and the new person in charge was promoted to inspector. The troublesome corporal was moved a few months later.

Every detachment had its own unique situation. We had detachments in industrial communities, rural farm areas, heavy tourist towns, such as, Jasper, Banff, and remote outposts such as Fort Chippaiwan, plus traffic units on freeways. This northerly detachment of Fort Chippaiwan had a population mainly composed of native Indians and was policed by a married corporal, and a single constable. Access from the outside was by air only. During my visit I had a very enjoyable visit and lunch with the corporal, his wife and one child. They both expressed their happiness at being at Fort Chippaiwan but asked that they be considered for a move in about a year for their child's schooling.

Edmonton Subdivision was very large and awkward to manage. The vast territory and large number of personnel did not permit proper monitoring of the work at each detachment, nor was it possible to know the members in order to make a proper assessment. Plans were being drawn up to break the subdivision down into four smaller units and to have their individual headquarters located out of Edmonton closer to the action. This plan was carried out in 1976 when the Commanding Officer retired to pension. The officer in charge of criminal investigation was promoted to assistant commissioner and placed as the commanding officer of 'K' Division (Alberta). My position became redundant and I was moved to the position of Officer-in-Charge of Criminal Investigation and second in charge of 'K' Division (Alberta). I was now responsible for all criminal investigations within Alberta including traffic, liquor, drugs, custom and immigration violations and homicide. This position is now called Criminal Operations Officer.

Chapter 18

Officer in Charge Criminal Investigation

'K' Division, Alberta

1976 to 1979

I found that this new position carried a great deal of responsibility, as I had meetings with the attorney general of Alberta or his assistant with respect to matters of criminal law. During my tenure I did not have any provincial political interference in our investigations.

The XI Commonwealth Games were scheduled for Edmonton in 1978 with preparation starting several years in advance. I was appointed director of security, with Inspector Ron McIntyre as my assistant, for the overall control of all security for visiting dignitaries, athletes, accommodation, transportation and venue sites. The Queen and Prince Phillip would be in attendance, as well as Prime Minister Trudeau and over twenty prime ministers of the commonwealth nations. The planning required the co-operation of the Edmonton City Police, the Canadian Armed Forces, additional manpower from our surrounding detachments in Alberta and additional back-up from our neighbouring provinces. There were thousands of volunteers who had to be screened for security plus all the game officials and the media. The co-operation by all was absolutely phenomenal.

During the majority of the games I was closeted in our command room, or as I referred to it, "the bunker." All matters related to security passed through the staff at this location. Margaret and I were able to attend the impressive opening and closing ceremonies and also the veladrome for the cycle races. The Commonwealth Games were a complete success and the game officials, athletes, dignitaries, volunteers, police and Armed Forces were pleased with the entire affair. Needless to say my staff and I were happy with the outcome, as we had had many months of planning and were constantly alert during the games for any problem.

An interesting sidelight to the security of the games arose just prior to their commencement. The Oil Minister for Saudi Arabia was due to arrive in Edmonton for a conference and we were to provide a token security. He was approached and his cooperation and asked if he had any objections to us providing a full security with limousine and escorts and all as a practice for the games. He agreed and our escort met him at the airport and escorted him into Edmonton via the lieutenant Governor's residence to his hotel. This was a worthwhile exercise as we were providing the same for all the heads of state. A later debriefing revealed some flaws which were corrected.

Various investigations arose during my tenure. There was a native blockade to the dam access on the Old Man River near Pincher Creek in the southern part of the province. After some tension-filled days of negotiation, the blockade was withdrawn. Another time a couple and their two children were camping in Elk Island National Park, their nine year old disappeared. An extensive manhunt was carried out for over a week, with the Army assisting, but absolutely no trace of the missing boy was found. We suspected the parents of foul play, but our investigation did not reveal a shred of evidence to support this theory. To date the boy has not been found.

By the summer of 1979 my tenure as member of the Royal Canadian Mounted Police was drawing to a close. When I had completed thirty years and six months with the Force plus four years and six months in the Royal Canadian Air Force, I had reached the required thirty-five years of service and must retire. I was at this time fifty-five years of age. Stella Lee, my very efficient and thoughtful secretary, quietly organized a staff farewell retirement party for me to be held in the mess. Margaret, Pat and Bruce, our daughter and son, attended with me and we were joined by the staff whom I had worked with for four years. They presented me with an engraved plaque and other gifts along with many kind speeches. I felt indeed delighted and humble. These people were dedicated, loyal, and genuinely sincere. I shall continue to have fond memories of them and my experiences in the Force.

My life in the Force had been very fulfilling with many adventures and lifelong friendships made. I sincerely enjoyed police work because of its diversity. You were expected to maintain the Federal Laws of Canada, the Provincial Statutes and the Municipal By-laws in the area where you resided. Investigation of every type of crime was involved from murder, bank robbery, drug enforcement, family disputes, motor vehicle accidents and a host of other offences that brought one into contact with the seamy side of humanity. On the other side of the coin, one experienced the satisfaction of helping people who were having a serious problem with one thing or another and the heartfelt gratitude they expressed for the assistance you rendered.

In the foregoing I have endeavoured to give the reader a cross-section of the many and numerous tasks, adventures and situations that a member of the R.C.M.Police is confronted with over the years. It is not possible to write about every encounter but I trust what I have covered may have spurred your interest.

I was proud to serve for over thirty years and I trust I made my contribution to its colourful history. I thoroughly enjoyed my time in the organization, its great people, and the constant challenges every day. Members of the Force came from all walks of life, from coast to coast in Canada, and from overseas. You trained with these members, worked with them and made acquaintances during your travels. I found all members, with rare exception, to be devoted to their work. I had a favourite saying to members in the Force: "You only get out of the organization what you have put into it." Many of these people possessed exceptional investigative skills that brought about very successful conclusions to extremely difficult and complicated cases. Any member who showed indications of being a slacker while under my command was monitored very closely and given adequate warnings in writing, and if there was no improvement, he was recommended for discharge. Fortunately, these situations were few and far between.

Do I feel I personally made a contribution to the Force during my tenure? Without any equivocation I can answer affirmatively. When entering the police I had four and one half years in the Air Force where you learn to work with others regardless of rank. Team work was required at all times in any endeavour. I would always say, "I worked with him or her," but never, "He or she worked for me." During my service I came close to being shot several times. When at Vernon, the situation with William Galko was extremely tense and could have ended in tragedy had the wrong words been uttered or a false move made. There was the situation at Grand Forks Detachment with Remezoff is a classical example of a person who decided to take the law into his own hands and almost caused serious injury or death by gun fire for three of the detachment members. Aggressive action by all members and a civilian helped bring this volatile situation to a close with the only casualty being the perpetrator himself. I received two commendations during my career, one from the Commanding Officer for an investigation in Vernon and the other from the Commissioner for bravery in saving the lives of two members at Grand Forks.

I feel that my foresight in identifying shortcomings in investigative areas has assisted the Force in implementing programs and systems that have proven effective to the investigator then and even now. The Special 'O' Section has proven its worth time after time. I spoke to Deputy Commissioner Proke, then Commanding Officer of British Columbia, while attending a function and he advised that Special 'O' surveillance groups are worth their weight in gold. The special services section that looks after all investigators' technical needs is functioning extremely well. The Special Internal Investigation group is still in existence at this date.

Any time you read of a member being investigated on an internal matter, it is this group conducting the inquiries who ensure that no bias enters into the probe. In closing I must at this time give credit to my superiors, for without their support these programs would have been placed in a filing cabinet and forgotten. All of these people, Commissioner Nadon, Deputy Commissioner Jack Ross, Deputy Commissioner Peter Bazowski and Assistant Commissioner Ed Willis and my staff, plus many others, assisted me greatly over the years. Because of their extensive police background and understanding, they could see the value in these new programs and the need for implementing them. I am indeed grateful.

There are of course those individuals who worked with me on these various projects, the other officers, non-commissioned officers, secretaries, clerical, and technical staff, plus those who actually carried out the programs with a determination that made them work. It is each individual's contribution, which in his or her own way has made the Royal Canadian Mounted Police an outstanding success for over one hundred and twenty-five years. I personally am honoured to have served in the Force and with its many individuals over the last thirty and a half years.

I have rambled on for these pages patting myself on the back and filling paragraphs full of accolades. The real support I received in the background was from my wonderful wife Margaret who put up with my long absences while on trips and late hours while on the job at home. During our time on the smaller detachments, in the absence of members from the office, she would answer the phones, operate the radio, deal with the public and prepare meals for the prisoners. She shouldered the responsibility of running a house over these past years and going through the hassle of transfers, raising the children, Pat and Bruce, and supervising their education in three provinces, as she carried on nursing at the local hospitals on a part-time basis. She had no easy task and I have to say the end result is the children are now grown up and have brought five delightful grandchildren into our family.

The most important event of all this history, after going through thick and thin with me for almost fifty-five years, is my dear wife, who is still with me enjoying the fruits of retirement, which she justly deserves.

37. Greeting visiting policemen from several African countries who came to study security procedure for the Commonwealth Games at Edmonton, Alberta. (R.C.M.Police photo)

38. R.C.M.Police helicopter ready to take me, Margaret and a visitor from England for a check of the sport venues at the Commonwealth Games.

210

39. Daily briefing session for the staff in preparation for a day of security measures. (R.C.M.Police photo)

40. Receiving updated reports on security activities during the Commonwealth Games. A large number of heads of state including Queen Elizabeth and members of the Royal Family all require police escort and security while attending the various venues. Security was also provided for the athletes to and from their activities including the villages. (R.C.M.Police photo)

41. Eventually comes retirement. Inspector Ron McIntyre presenting me with a gift onbehalf of the Criminal Investigation staff. Looking on are Margaret on my left, Stella Lee my secretary, and Heather Conroy another staff member.
(R.C.M.Police photo)

ODE TO THE C.I.B. OFFICER

There are so many things I'd like
To tell you face to face,
I either lack the words or fail
To find the time or place.

But in this special letter, Sir,
You'll find, at least in part,
The feelings that the past year,
Have left within my heart.

The memories of our C.I.B. days
And all that you have done,
To make the office a happy place
And working so much fun.

This letter comes to thank you, Sir,
For needed words and praise,
The counsel and guidance, too,
That shaped up my secretarial days.

No words of mine can tell you
The things I really feel
But you must know my respect for you
Is warm, lasting, and real.

You made my world a better place
And through the coming years,
I'll keep the C.I.B. memories of you
As cherished souvenirs.

Stella Lee

79 JUN 22   Stella LEE

42. This young lady was my secretary and a person you would be proud
    to have on your staff. She had foresight, she was thoughtful and
    efficient, and, above all, was always cheerful and considerate of other
    staff members. Stella was born in Switzerland and raised in Canada;
    I called her the 'Swiss Miss" which I think she enjoyed. The above
    letter took me by complete surprise and I am honoured with her
    sincere and kind thoughts.

43. Picture taken at the same farewell. The author (left centre) with
     some department heads (left to right) Corporal Pat Timms,
     staff sergeants George Flake, George Leggitt, Ed Rouleau, and
     Grant Eppy. I must say I was blessed with a wonderful crew of
     people, great way to end a thirty year career.
     (R.C.M.Police photo)

44. Margaret and I with the Captain of the S.S. *Rotterdam* while on a Carribbean cruise. (Holland America photo)

45. After retirement we still attended air force and police functions.
We are at the Chilliwack Subdivision ball. From left to right;
the author, Assistant Commissioner Ed Willes (Retired), Deputy
Commissioner Don Wilson Commanding Officer "E" Division,
BritishColumbia and Assistant Commission Ed Witherden (Retired).
(R.C.M.Police photo)

Chapter 19

Chairman of the Driver Control Board

Province of Alberta

1979 to 1984

Back at it! Nearing the end of my career with the R.C.M. Police I was advised by a person in the Alberta Solicitor General's office, that of the Chairman of the Driver Control Board would be coming vacant as soon as the incumbent retired, I was asked to consider applying for the position, which I did. After the usual interview process by the Deputy Solicitor General, I was selected and entered into the service of the Alberta Government at the same pay scale I had been receiving from the Federal Government.

Upon commencement I had a lengthy briefing from the Deputy Minister who advised he was now in a position to upgrade the Driver Control Board, a move that was sorely needed. He wanted its stature or image in the eyes of the public to be raised, as the body was a quasi-judicial organization. He gave me six months to get settled into the position, make an assessment of what was required and bring the suggestions to him. This assessment was to include personnel, the Statute governing the Board, office space, filing system, budget and the possibility of implementing a computer system. In other words, a complete make-over as and where required.

The Driver Control Board was established by the Alberta Government in an attempt to reduce the number of motor vehicle violations from Motor Vehicle to Criminal Code driving offences. The Board's activities were initiated by the Motor Vehicle Division as they identified frequent violators and forwarded the driving records to us. The Driver Control Board was an entirely separate entity from the Motor Vehicle Division even though we were in the same office tower in down-town Edmonton. Upon receipt of his or her file, the driver would be summoned to the Board by registered letter requiring them to appear with or without a lawyer on a stated date, time and place.

I have to admit I was fairly surprised by the general appearance of the office. Desks were crammed together, and files were everywhere in cardboard boxes and filing cabinets that occupied every spare space in the office. The appearance was certainly not what you would expect to see in a quasi-judicial setting that catered to a large volume of the public. The office was crowded with five clerical staff, one administrative assistant and three board members all endeavouring to work amid a scene of cramped space and clutter. The hearings were held in one of the board members' offices and it was difficult to get five to six people in one office.

I was warmly welcomed by all the staff, with the exception of a senior board member. He apparently resented my being the new chairman as he had applied for the position. The other board member by the name of Len Anderson, who had a Degree in Divinity and was an ordained minister proved to be a loyal, dedicated assistant and a gentleman. He came forward to help plus he explained the inner workings to make me familiar with the office and staff. I had a one-on-one interview with all the staff and they seemed pleased with what had transpired but all were overworked because of sheer volume. The one unhappy board member decided to take holidays and upon his return announced he was quitting and going into the dog kennel business on his acreage outside of Edmonton. He had a degree in psychology, but somehow it did not help his demeanour.

Since the Board held hearings throughout the province, a great deal of time was spent in travel. The case load was equal in numbers in the southern half of the province as it was in the northern portion. The sum and substance of my first six months was a report to the Deputy

Minister for the opening of a Driver Control Board office in Calgary and the appointment of three new board members and the necessary clerical staff. I also recommended the office in Edmonton be enlarged for the staff, plus a separate board room for hearings, as well as additional administrative assistants in Edmonton, Grand Prairie, Calgary and Lethbridge. These positions were counsellors to interview offending drivers under the age of 18 years. Last but not least, I asked for an entirely new filing system to be included in the computer study presently under- way for the Motor Vehicle Division. The entire report was discussed in full with the Deputy Minister and he accepted my recommendations. They were implemented over the next two years.

The board member who quit in protest over my appointment came back in two years asking for his job back. Apparently his kennel business was a failure and he was looking for some income. After an interview he was advised he could come back only as a board member, as Len Anderson was now vice chairman. The Deputy agreed to my suggestion and this chap was re-hired. I am relating this story as it leads to some humorous incidents.

As I mentioned, he lived on an acreage which was blessed with poplar trees of the kind that shed the white, fluffy seeds. One night we had a thunderstorm and his old car was sitting by his house with all the windows open and it filled with fluff. The next day he drove to work, and when he arrived at the office he was the most dishevelled looking mess you ever laid eyes on. He always had a beard and his hair a little on the long side and he wore a heavy tweed jacket, and when he walked into the office he was covered entirely with fluffy white seeds that had blown around in his car. He did not seem concerned and went straight to his office and started to work. The office staff couldn't believe their eyes. He was to hold hearings very shortly, but gave no indication of cleaning himself of the fluff on his hair, beard or jacket. I had to call him in and tell him to tidy himself up which he did, but at the same time he was laughing about his behaviour commenting he did not think it was that bad.

He went to Calgary one winter week-end with his family and on his return he related how he had run into a blizzard north of Red Deer and shortly afterwards got a flat tire. The temperature was around minus 20 degrees Celsius with a wind chill factor much lower. He had no coat, nor gloves and attempted to change the tire. After jacking the car up, he took the wheel nuts off but it got so cold he had to jump into the car and warm up, then continue. His hands began to freeze and he took off his socks and used them as gloves. He is very fortunate he did not suffer frost-bite with that type of exposure or worse still, the entire family freeze to death. He was very unconcerned while relating this story, and we were all amazed he was telling us of his near brush with death in such a humorous vein. I asked him if he ever carried a winter survival kit in his car as most Albertans did, but he said he never thought of that. Yes, he was the classic example of the absent- minded professor.

Our Minister, Solicitor General Graham Harle, was from Camrose. He was not in my opinion a particularly forceful individual. He never bothered the Board in any way but did some peculiar things. At about 2 a.m. one morning he was found by the Edmonton City Police Vice Squad in a room with a prostitute in the skid row area of the city. He was asked to identify himself and he explained he was in this situation because he was doing a study into prostitution on behalf of his department. I must say the media had a field day with this matter and the premier was very embarrassed. Mr. Harle was forced to resign his portfolio and he returned to his law practice in Camrose.

I enjoyed my five years with the Driver Control Board having had a great staff who worked hard to bring about the best results. Despite some adverse media and public comment, public servants on the whole are a dedicated and hard-working group. There were, of course, exceptions, as some personnel were not ambitious and were just plain lazy or incompetent. There was a saying that if you wanted to fire a person in the Alberta Government you needed an act of parliament to do so because of the union. Some of these poor performers would be pushed from Corrections to the Motor Vehicle Division to the Driver Control Board and other departments. Those in charge of these departments were always lobbying the deputy ministers to get these deadheads out of their operation into a vacancy in another department. I was constantly on the alert for this activity and would fight it verbally all the way, but I was not always successful.

In August, 1984, after 5 years service, Deputy Minister Rheal LeBlanc and all the heads of departments in the Solicitor General's Ministry staged a retirement party for me which was excellent. I have to say I was very honoured and after the speeches, jokes and presentation we had a hilarious time.

Thus ended my working career spanning forty-four years. My life in the work force included four and one half years in the R.C.A.F. starting in 1940, carried through various post-war occupations prior to the R.C.M.Police, and ended with the Province of Alberta Driver Control Board. Margaret and I had now to decide where our retirement was going to take us next. It was by no means an easy decision.

However, we decided to move back to Vernon, our first posting in the B.C. Provincial Police and an area with which we were very familiar. The countryside was beautiful, winters were quite mild and the general climate was semi-arid, not like the west coast with its monsoon season from November to March each year. We bought a piece of land overlooking the lake and hills, where we can watch the length of the lake and any thing that happened on or around. Margaret and I designed our house to accommodate my model railroad, and studio for Margaret an aspiring artist. She spent years painting the vistas and enjoyed being part of a local group of artists. I was until recently, active in the local model railroad club and other organizations. Since our retirement we have been very busy with hobbies and other activities. I have been asked what do I do in my spare time, my response is simply, fight cancer.

Over the ensuing years, I and many other veterans have noticed a decline in recognition by Canada of those who served in the Second World War and in particular Royal Air Force Bomber Command who made a major contribution to the freedom and life style that we all enjoy regardless of ethnic background. There is a certain element of the media, including our own Canadian Broadcasting Corporation and the National Film Board, who readily broadcast this distorted material from so-called historians who attempt to write historical material only as they perceive it. This is done without any thought as to how untrue or offensive their material is, or the repercussions it has on those who really know the true facts and participated in this historical event. It is for this reason I have undertaken these memoirs as my small contribution to the literary world along with many other persons who have previously written genuine historical articles. I trust this account of my World War II service along with the material in the Appendix C will bring some balance to the picture. I also hope that my years of Canadian policing will give the reader a greater insight and support for the organizations I served for nearly half of my life.

Margaret and I are extremely proud of Canada and its' citizens. Bless you all!

Appendix A

Awards and Decorations

1. Citation for the award of the Distinguished Flying Cross
    as submitted by Group Captain Reginald Lane,
    Commanding Officer, 405 Squadron in 1944. The flying
    hours for each sortie are shown.

2. An illustration of the British Commonwealth Orders,
    Decorations and Medals.

3. The Distinguish Flying Cross and number issued during
    various conflicts.

ROUTLEDGE, P/O John Denison (J19988)

DISTINGUISHED FLYING CROSS – 49 Squadron (R.A.F.) & No. 405 Squadron (R.C.A.F.)(Pathfinder)

Award effective 19 June 1944 as per London Gazette dates 27 June 1944 and AFRO 1861/44 dated 25 August 1944. Born Mission City, British Columbia, 1922; home there. Trained at No.7 BGS and No.2 WS. Commissioned 1944. No citation other than "completed....many successful operations against the enemy in which [he has] displayed high skill, fortitude and devotion to duty." Public Records Office Air 2/8780 has recommendation by W/C R.J. Lane dated 23 March 1944 when he had flown 51 sorties (322 hours 50 minutes) as follows:

49 Squadron (R.A.F.)			
20 June 42	Dinghy search, * Frisian Isls. (6.15)	17 Jan 43	Berlin (7.00)
11 Aug 41	NICKELLING, Vichy Fr. (7.25)	27 Jan 43	Dusseldorf (5.30)
15 Aug 42	GARDENING, Frisian Isls. (4.00)	30 Jan 43	Hamburg (6.30)
27 Aug 42	Kassel (4.55)	1 Feb 43	Wilhelmshaven (5.55)
28 Aug 42	Nuremburg (6.40)	13 Feb 43	Lorient Fr. (6.40)
6 Sept 42	Duisburg (4.00)	**405 Squadron (R.C.A.F.)**	
8 Sept 42	Frankfurt (6.25)	20 Dec 43	Frankfurt (5.20)
10 Sept 42	Dusseldorf (4.20)	23 Dec 43	Berlin (7.30)
13 Sept 42	Bremen (4.10)	29 Dec 43	Berlin (6.10)
14 Sept 42	Wilhelmshaven (4.10)	1 Jan 44	Berlin (6.55)
16 Sept 42	Essen (4.55)	5 Jan 44	Stettin (9.10)
18 Sept 42	GARDENING, Gulf of Danzig (9.45)	20 Jan 44	Berlin (7.10)
23 Sept 42	Wismar (6.15)	21 Jan 44	Magdeburg (6.45)
24 Sept 42	GARDNENING, Kullen (7.25)	27 Jan 44	Berlin (7.15)
1 Oct 42	Wismar (6.15)	28 Jan 44	Berlin (7.30)
13 Oct 42	Kiel (5.35)	30 Jan 44	Berlin(6.00)
15 Oct 42	Cologne (4.50)	15 Feb 44	Berlin (6.40)
17 Oct 42	Le Creusot Fr. (10.15)*	25 Feb 44	Augsburg (6.45)
22 Oct 42	Genoa It. (9.25)	1 Mar 44	Stuttgart (6.55)
24 Oct 42	Milan It. (9.35) *	15 Mar 44	Stuttgart (6.30)
15 Nov 42	Genoa It. (8.10)	18 Mar 44	Frankfurt (4.50)
28 Nov 42	Turin It. (8.40)	24 Mar 44	Frankfurt (5.00)
8 Dec 42	Turin It. (8.10)	30 Mar 44	Nurenburg (6.50)
9 Dec 42	Turin It. (3.15), (early return)	18 Apr 44	Tergnier Fr. (3.05)
20 Dec 42	Duisburg(4.35)	20 Apr 44	Lens Fr. (2.05)
16 Jan 43	Berlin (7.25)	24 Apr 44	Karlesruhe (5.40)
		*indicates Daylight sortie	

This officer is a highly efficient Air Gunner who has completed 51 operational sorties against such heavily defended enemy targets as Berlin, Frankfurt and Stettin. In the face of extreme danger this officer has shown courage of a high order and has not been deterred from successfully completing his missions. His fine example has been an inspiration to those less experienced than himself and to the squadron in general. Strongly recommended for the award of the Distinguished Flying Cross.

For Honour and Valour

Commonwealth Orders, Decorations and Medals awarded to RCAF Personnel during the Second World War

All information on these pages comes from Canadian Orders, Decorations and Medals, by Surgeon Commander F.J. Blatherwick, The Unitrade Press, 1983. Permission gratefully acknowledged.

The Distinguished Flying Cross

Awarded to Officers and Warrant Officers for an act or acts of valour, courage, or devotion to duty performed whilst flying in active operations against the enemy.

Bars: For additional acts of bravery. Silver bar with an eagle in centre.

Obverse: Cross flory terminated in the horizontal and base bars with bombs, the upper bar terminating with a rose, surmounted by another cross composed of aeroplane propellers charged in the centre with a roundel within a wreath of laurels, a rose winged ensigned by an Imperial Crown, theron the letters RAF.

Description: Cross flory, 2 1/8 inches across, silver.

Reverse: Royal Cypher above the date 1918 in a circle, year of issue on lower arm.

Mounting: Ring at top of cross attached to the suspender by a small ring.

Ribbon: 1 1/4 inches; Violet and White alternate diagonal stripes 1/8" at 45 degrees left to right. The Violet colour is to appear in the bottom left and upper right corners when viewed on the wearer's chest. Until 1919, the stripes were horizontal.

Total Issued as of 1983:

- WWI -- 193 + 9 bars.
- WWII -- 4018 + 214 bars + 5 second bars.
- Korea -- 1 to RCAF plus 1 to Canadian Army. (FIL Glover and Capt. Tees)

Example

A/C Jonny Fauquier, D.S.O. and two Bars, D.F.C., Croix de Guerre with Palm, Legion of Honour--- King of the Dambusters; the first RCAF Officer and non-Briton to command an RAF bomber squadron, 617 Squadron.

Appendix B

Minelaying

Minelaying by aircraft was given the code name "Gardening."

The following illustrates how the code names were derived;
the oceans and seas around Europe were segregated and
charted into areas and each given the name of a fruit,
vegetable, or flower.

Statistics reveal minelaying from aircraft at low altitude over
water, at night, was quite hazardous.

These statistics are displayed with the permission of Larry
T.Wright, a member of the Bomber Command Historians.

Code Names for Minelaying Areas (1940-45)

Anemones	Le Havre
Artichokes	Lorient
Asparagus	Great Belt
Barnacle	Zeebrugee
Beech	St. Nazaire
Bottle	Haugesund
Broccoli	Great Belt
Carrots	Little Belt
Cinnamon	La Rochelle
Cypress	Dunkirk
Daffodil	The Sound
Deodar	Bordeaux
Dewberry	Boulogne
Eglantine	Heligoland
Elderberry	Bayonne
Endives	Little Belt
Flounder	Maas and Scheldt
Forget-me-nots	Kiel Canal
Furze	St. Jean De Luz
Hawthorne	Esberg Approaches
Hollyhock	Trevemunde
Hyacinth	St. Malo
Geranium	Swinemunde
Gorse	Quiberon
Greengage	Cherbourg
Jasmine	Trevemunde
Jellyfish	Brest
Juniper	Antwerp
Krauts	Lim Fjord
Lettuces	Kiel Canal
Limpets	Den Helder
Melon	Kiel Canal
Mullet	Spezia
Mussels	Terschilling Gat
Nasturtiums	The Sound

Nectarines	Frisian Islands
Newt	Maas Scheldt
Onions	Rotterdam
Prawns	Calais
Privet	Danzig
Pumpkins	Great Belt
Quinces	Great Belt
Quinces	Kiel Bay
Radishes	Kiel Bay
Rosemary	Heligoland
Scallops	Rouen
Silverthorne	Kattegat areas
Sweet peas	Rostock and Arcone Light
Tangerine	Pillau
Tomato	Oslo Fjord approaches
Trefoils	Texal (South)
Turbot	Ostend
Undergrowth	Kattegat
Verbena	Copenhagen approaches
Vine Leaves	Dieppe
Wallflowers	Kiel Bay
Whelks	Zuider Zee
Willow	Arcona ro R. Dievenow
Zeranthemums	R. Jade
Yewtree	Kattegat
Zinneas	R. Jade

Bomber Command Minelaying (Sea) Statistics

February 1943 to May 1945

1942	Aircraft Dispatched	Aircraft Missing	Number of Mines Laid
Up to February	2716	57	2185
March	3027	68	2541
April	3771	78	3110
May	3821	94	4133
June	4337	103	5300
July	4771	114	6197
August	5153	130	7165
September	5621	147	8266
October	6082	161	9248
November	6664	176	10404
December	7085	183	11391
Totals	53048	1331 or 2.47%	69940

1943	Aircraft Dispatched	Aircraft Missing	Number of Mines Laid
January	7681	199	12676
February	8221	208	13805
March	8732	226	14964
April	9423	259	16833
May	9791	267	17981
June	10217	274	19155
July	10530	280	20082
August	11032	290	21185
September	11429	293	22373
October	11796	298	23449
November	12148	306	24425

December	12404	311	25225
Totals	123404	3211 or 2.60%	232153

1944	Aircraft Dispatched	Aircraft Missing	Number of Mines Laid
January	12777	314	26326
February	13547	323	27987
March	14065	326	29459
April	14919	345	32102
May	15745	354	34862
June	16205	355	36640
July	16389	357	37348
August	16803	369	38934
September	16988	373	39682
October	17245	381	40815
November	17415	382	41565
December	17675	385	42725
Totals	189773	4264 or 2.25%	428445

1945	Aircraft Dispatched	Aircraft Missing	Number of Mines Laid
January	17834	391	43393
February	18126	400	44747
March	18402	405	45945
April	18682	408	47307
May	19025	408	47307
Totals	92069	2012 or 2.19%	228699

Overall Totals	458294	10798 or 2.36%	959237

Appendix C

Extract from the book " *So Many.*"

"50 Years On"

By

Bill Gunston   John Goley

Nearly fifty years after the Battle of Britain, silhouette artist Michael Pierce told Air Chief Marshal Sir Harry Broadhurst that he was seeking a way to honour the pilots who won that crucial battle. "Great idea," said Sir Harry, "but don't forget Bomber Command." In due course a unique book was created, entitled...*So Few*. It told the stories of 25 survivors who helped win the head-on contest against Hitler's Luftwaffe, and thereby stave off invasion and irrevocable defeat. The 25 urged us to go on and produce a companion volume honouring Bomber Command. Their collective opinions were that for sheer determined courage under dreadful conditions of cold, fatigue and constant mortal danger, nothing could surpass the example of their brothers-in-arms in Bomber Command.

We produced 401 copies of *So Few*, each priced at 1600 pounds, and designed to look almost new after several hundred years. W.H.Smith, Britain's biggest book retailer, then followed with a popular edition, made from normal high-quality book materials, which for several weeks, was number 3 in the non-fiction best seller list. But we never forgot what we promised; you now have the companion volume, entitled "*So Many.*" This has been produced to honour the far greater number of air crew who in World War

Two flew with Bomber Command of the Royal Air Force, and also the men and women who in the harshest of conditions magnificently supported them on the ground.

Bomber Command was formed in July 1936. At that time the biplanes were about to be replaced by much faster monoplanes, fitted with power-driven turrets, intended to offer defensive firepower in all directions. Their introduction was not without difficulty. They were heavier, took off and landed faster than their predecessors. Grass fields had to be replaced with long paved runways, and pilots had to be reminded not to land with the wheels retracted. Because of their cost and demanding nature the Blenheim, Whitley, Hampden and Wellington were flown infrequently, almost always in daytime. It was confidently believed that a tight formation of them could fight their way in daylight to an enemy target and back.

Bomber Command operated against Germany from the first day of World War 2. It was not allowed to drop bombs, except on units of the German fleet, so small forces of the latest bombers would cross the North Sea and search for German warships. The RAF was completely unaware of the fact that the Germans were busy installing air-defence radar, but they repeatedly found that daylight raids were suicidal.

On the 18th of December, a formation of 24 Wellingtons   was intercepted by fighters off the German coast; ten were quickly shot down, and only three returned unscathed. This at last convinced the Air Staff that not even a well-disciplined formation of modern bombers could survive in daylight. But to switch to night operations was a daunting prospect because it had not been planned for. The RAF Manual of Navigation, a substantial tome, had little to say about night navigation except it would be "performed by the light of towns." Not only did crews have no experience in flying at night over blacked-out countryside but they seldom flew at night at all. One crew member in this book recalls

"On my first operational flight I doubled my night-flying hours."

The RAF remained blissfully ignorant of its actual performance. In 1941 HM Stationery Office published a book *Bomber Command,* to show how successful the British Bombers were. It took the reader behind the scenes at a briefing: "The target is the synthetic oil plant at Gelsenkirchen...The most vital section of this plant is the hydrogenation plant, marked 'B'...a direct hit with a large bomb on the compressor house would..." This book boosted the morale of the much bombed British public, who were to read how the RAF was hitting back. The truth was somewhat different.

On the 19th of March, 1940, when the only targets the RAF was allowed to bomb were the German fleet and its bases, 50 aircraft took off to bomb the naval base at Sylt, a large and distinctive island. On return, 41 crews reported that they had bombed successfully, but subsequent photo-reconnaissance failed to reveal a single bomb crater! The idea of selecting as a target the compressor house in an oil plant at Gelsenkirchen was nonsense because at night few crews could even find that city. On the 18th of November 1940, it was reported that 262 tons of bombs had been dropped on Gelsenkirchen's two oil plants. Subsequent reconnaissance showed no damage to these installations whatsoever.

The Prime Minister's scientific advisor thought it was about time Bomber Command's results were examined in a cold analytical manner. The resulting Butt Report of August 1941, concluded that on average one-third of all crews failed to get anywhere near the target area. Of those who did claim to have bombed the target, only one-third actually got within five miles of it. In the attacks on the misty Ruhr, heart of the Nazi war industry, the proportion was below one-tenth, and on moonless nights even easy targets scored about one-fifteenth.

The fault lay not in the skill or dedication but in the inadequate methods. Ever since 1936 various electronic navigation aids had been suggested, including radar which could "paint a picture of the ground," and guidance based on signals sent from stations in England. Little had been done, though in 1940 the ability of the Luftwaffe crews to bomb every major city in Great Britain had been found to rest on a precision system of guidance beams called Knickebein, which did not even require a special receiver in the aircraft. (The signal was received by the Lorenz bad-weather landing aid.)

On the 23rd of February, 1942, Air Marshal Sir Arthur Harris was appointed C-in-C of Bomber Command. The morale began to improve at once. When he took over, the twin engined "heavies" were being replaced by the bigger Sterling, Halifax and Lancaster. Equally important, the Telecommunications Research Establishment was at last developing electronic aids that would enable the crews to find their targets.

First came Gee, which covered the northwest Europe with an invisible lattice of intersecting signals sent from three stations in south-east England. Using a special receiver and charts, the bomber navigator always knew where he was within a kilometre or so. In December, 1942, in the teeth of the opposition from the people who could not understand it, came the most precise of all, Oboe. Again relying on signals from Britain, out to a radius of some 400 km (250miles), this could guide an aircraft with an accuracy of some 100 meters.

In January, 1943, bombers began using radar which painted a picture of the ground. Called H2S, it was heavy, disrupted bomber production and made it impossible to fit a turret or even a window to defend against a night fighter underneath. Unknown to the RAF, this is where the most dangerous fighters were going to be – and it behaved like a lighthouse, broadcasting the bomber's position to those same night fighters. It was also extremely difficult to use, but it had an advantage that it could not be jammed by the enemy, went wherever the bomber went and, in the hands of a skilled operator, enabled bombs or TIs (pyrotechnic target indicators) to be dropped accurately even over unbroken mist or cloud.

Clearly, what was needed was to fit these aids to special marker aircraft, which could put down unambiguous TIs as aiming points for the Main Force. After much argument this was sanctioned, and the PFF (Pathfinder Force) began operating from August, 1942. Their marking by Lancasters using H2S and Mosquitoes with Oboe absolutely transformed Bomber Command's Operations. As the striking power of the force grew, so did Harris's leadership not only keep morale sky-high but he insisted on trying to get more aircraft over the target in the shortest time, and thus saturating the defences and allowing more aircraft to return unscathed. Achieving a concentrated bomber stream was assisted by putting down TIs on the way as route markers.

Increasingly, the war in the German night sky became one not only of human courage and skill but also of science. After both sides had refrained from using it for fear that the enemy might do likewise, in the summer of 1943 Bomber Command began dispensing billions of strips of tin foil, called "Window" (today known as Chaff), to fill the sky with reflectors that would smother the enemy's radar displays. Soon high-power electronic jammers were bought into play, until the RAF formed 100 Group whose sole function was to use more advanced technology to interfere with the German defences.

The results were that Bomber Command's attacks, initially a mere nuisance, became what Hitler's armament minister Albert Speer called "the greatest battle we lost." On 14 May, 1940, one "kampfgeschwader" (bomber group of the Luftwaffe) systematically bombed Rotterdam, while the surrender of the city was being negotiated. Churchill, who had been prime minister for only four days, at once told the RAF it could at last drop bombs on Germany. On the next night 93 bombers set out for Krupp Works at Essen. In a later assessment it was calculated that the proportion of bombs to actually hit the vast factories was 3 percent. In contrast, in a massive attack by 705 "heavies" on the 25th of July, 1943, marked by Oboe-equipped Pathfinders, the proportion was assessed at 96 per cent.

Having dwelt at length on navigation, a little should be said about other crew members. The flight engineer was a vital link between the air crew and the ground crews, and his duties are outlined in the story of Lyndom Sims. The bomber aimer lay prone in the nose, where he had the best view ahead, and helped with pinpointing and navigating. Approaching the target, he set up the Mk XIV bombsight to take account of variables of height, airspeed, wind and different bomb trajectories. After "Bomb Doors Open," he gave the pilot steering instructions over the intercom, left...left...steady... right a little" – so the target could be seen approaching along precisely the desired relative path. When it reached the drop point he pressed a hand-held switch, releasing the bombs in predetermined sequence. Then "Bomb Doors Closed," a quick check for hang-ups and then he squeezed into the front turret to help with night fighter defence. The term "signaller" was coined in 1942 to identify the operator of communications radio, and the newly introduced electronic aids to navigation and bombing. Previously they had been WO/Ags, wireless air gunners who were also trained as gunners. The mid-upper and rear gunners had the unenvied positions in draughty cold and claustrophobic turrets. Most turrets were of the Frazer-Nash type, rotated and with guns elevated or depressed by hydraulic power, the gunner having controls resembling motorcycle handle bars with safety grips and triggers on each. The Halifax had Boulton Paul turrets with electro-hydraulic drive and firing button on top of the control column like a fighter. Each turret was armed with two or four Browning machine guns. These guns were of 0.303-inch (7.7 mm) calibre the same as army rifles of the period. Skilled gunners did well, provided the enemy came close enough, but they were far out ranged by the fighter's heavy destructive cannon. Early in the war some bombers had ventral turrets on the underside of the fuselage, but such turrets were soon discontinued. Later, the majority of the Bomber Command losses were caused by fighters fitted with an upward firing cannon, whose approach could not readily be seen by the crew.

This book *So Many* is not a history of Bomber Command's operations. It is an attempt to set down for future generations the kind of men who formed the crews, and who - if they thought about it – either knew that it was unlikely that they would survive the war or kidded themselves they were invincible. Most of them were boys straight from the school classroom, too young to vote in a government election. The turnover in crews was such that a steady stream came and vanished without any one on the squadron getting to know them. Those who disappeared were just as good as those who, by chance, managed to survive. Unless they were extraordinarily lucky, even the most expert crews would eventually have 'FTR' (failed to return) chalked up against their aircraft on a big blackboard in the briefing room.

In such an environment the camaraderie of the crew was crucial. Morale was sustained by the knowledge that one was part of the best crew in Bomber Command – which almost everyone believed he was. But every human eventually reaches the limit to the cumulative stress he can bear. This is discussed later in a professional overview.

Who were these air crew? Were they the same breed as today's 'lager louts'? In many squadrons anyone as old as 25 might be called grandpa, and have served as a father-confessor, or as a C.O. pass on the sad news to the next of kin. Family background counted for nothing. Ability, and the ability to inspire confidence in others, counted for everything. Over the years the R.A.F. had been constructing a filtering process which weeded out anyone whose confidence was superficial. Rare indeed was the crew who doubted the worth of one of their number. Integrity of the crew was sacrosanct. A crew with anyone in the slightest degree doubtful was swiftly reorganized. It was a matter of life or death. And not least of the remarkable factors is that the surviving crews, who became closely knit into a single instantly reacting unit, were made up of a mix of nationalities, ranks and family backgrounds.

Thus tens of thousands of young men from the United Kingdom and all parts of the British Empire, plus a few refugees from European countries, joined the R.A.F. after a short train journey, or after six weeks at sea, or desperately avoiding capture by Hitler's advancing war machine. On receipt into the RAF they would report via a reception centre to an initial training wing, where they would learn to stand up straight, march smartly and study classroom subjects. Quite often, the course had to include the English language as well as hygiene and sanitation, air force law, aircraft recognition, principles of flight, armaments and many other topics.

From the I.T.S (initial training school) those displaying no obvious shortcomings would find themselves at an E.F.T.S (elementary flying school), or on a ship heading for distant parts of the Empire or the U.S.A. In World War 2 the Empire (from 1942, Commonwealth) Air Training Plan trained over 75,000 pilots, 40,500 navigators, over 15,600 bomb aimers and nearly 38,000 air gunners, to the highest standards. Many thousand more were trained in the U.S.A.

R.A.F. air crew cadets wore airman uniform, with a distinguishing white flash in the front of their forage cap. They were expected to behave as young gentlemen, and at some schools the instructors might address their pupils as "Mr. Smith" or even "Sir," Training courses, so chaotic in World War I, were precise. Over the years the R.A.F. had learned which things were important. First impressions of each cadet might prove misleading, and several slow learners were to become a future Chief of Air Staff.

After primary or elementary stage, pupil pilots would be split into single or multi-engined. Or the gaping maw of

Bomber Command ensured that perhaps four out of five would be classed as 'multi.' Thus, thousands who joined in order to emulate the fighter pilots of the Battle of Britain found themselves at a Service Flying Training School flying twin- engined Oxfords, Anson or Cranes. Early in the war many pilots qualified with as few as 120 hours, but the vast wartime training scheme often gave pupils 220 hours over 18 months. Then at 'wings parade' they would change from being the lowest ranks in the RAF to being a Sergeant or a Pilot Officer.

The Commonwealth Air Training Plan was a rare example of strategic vision which was actually carried into effect. In the 1930s nobody could have foreseen that soon Britain would be isolated off the shore of a German-held continent, nor that it would be possible for Bomber Command to lose more than 500 air crew in a single night. The beleaguered wartime island could never have trained aircrew in anything remotely like the numbers needed. Yet it is surely remarkable that this gigantic plan by late 1944 had trained 131,553 air crew in Canada, 23,262 in Australia, 16,857 in South Africa, 8,235 in Southern Rhodesia, 3,891 in New Zealand and over 13,000 (all pilots) in the U.S.A. Most of this enormous output then came to Britain to be honed to operational standard.

Each newly qualified aircrew member would first report to an Operational Training Unit. For most of the war O.T.U.s were equipped with twin-engine aircraft which until 1942 had been the mainstay of Bomber Command. This was a big hurdle to surmount, partly because these aircraft were bigger and more powerful than anything encountered previously, and partly because, instead of vast areas of desert or scrub with a single road or railway, O.T.U. training missions were over densely populated country with hundreds of roads, dozens of railways, countless villages and towns, unpredictably foul weather and the omnipresent fear of enemy aircraft.

At O.T.U. the different air crew brevets would come together. Previously, those wearing a single wing with AG in the centre had been surrounded exclusively by other air gunners. Now they encountered those wearing N for navigator, E for engineer, B for bomb aimer, possibly the O for (observer) brevet of pre-1942 and double wings for the pilot. This motley collection would now be invited to 'crew up.'

This task was left to the men themselves. Sometimes they would march into the hangar and be told to get on with it. Sometimes the process took place bit by bit in the messes, classroom or bar of the local pub. With such a haphazard process one might expect problems. For example, how does a man of 19 assess the true worth of someone on whom his life may depend? Suffice to say the system worked. Many thousands of Bomber Command crews formed in the casual manner quickly became forged into the most indivisible entities. Crews tended to do everything together, and those that survived usually kept in touch in a lifelong relationship.

Invariably, the captain of the aircraft ('Skipper' to his crew) was the pilot. In the air his authority was unquestioned, though he might be a sergeant and the navigator, a squadron leader. Discipline was automatic, not enforced; each member of the crew was like a cog in a well-oiled machine, knowing precisely how to react to emergencies without waiting for commands or advice, but keeping others informed.

It may be difficult for people whose experience in flying has been in modern airliners or light aircraft to imagine the harshness of a wartime bomber. A Whitely pilot recalls, "Rain used to come into the cockpit, and for three months my hands were frost-bitten." Everywhere there was bare metal, with numerous sharp corners, and vital switches that were all too easy to brush against, especially when one's bulk was inflated by multiple layers of clothing needed to keep out the freezing cold, plus a yellow 'Mae West' around the upper body for flotation.

Today's hard helmets referred to as 'bone dome' had not been thought of. Instead a leather helmet covered the head, bulging with vital earphones. Goggles were issued but seldom needed. Except for the eyes, the face was covered by a carefully fitted mask which contained a microphone and life-giving oxygen. For the air gunners, one of the layers of clothing would be electrically heated, plugged into the aircraft supply,

Every man wore a parachute harness. The pilots might be permanently attached to the parachute, which formed a cushion on which to sit. All other crew would stow or hang their parachute packs in an allotted place, which in the case of the rear gunner might be just too far away in a crisis. Before abandoning the aircraft each man would grab his pack and clip it on steel hooks at the front of the harness.

From the O.T.U., usually via a short course at a Heavy Conversion Unit equipped with the type of aircraft they were to fly, crews were posted to an operational squadron. Long before the war, plans had been laid to replace twin-engined bombers with four-engined 'heavies.' The first of these was the Short Sterling, and although it did at first outstanding work, in the long term it proved a disappointment, complicated to build and maintain, unable to carry the later large bomb loads, and with such a low operating ceiling that it suffered a high casualty rate. Next came the Handley Page Halifax, which was progressively modified until it was in most respects a fine aircraft. The Avro Manchester proved to be simple to build and in many respects the best of all, but it was dangerously flawed by its two Vulture engines. When redesigned with four Rolls-Royce engines the result was the Lancaster, so good that Bomber Command's leader wanted every bomber factory to switch to making Lancasters only. Perhaps the only fault of the 'Lanc' was that it was difficult to escape from; of the crew of seven or eight the average number to get out was 1.7, compared with 2.45 for the Halifax.

When it was all over, of the men who flew with Bomber Command at the start of the war, over 90 per cent were killed. Even those who became operational after D-Day, 6th of June, 1944, suffered almost 50 per cent casualties. Many people, and certainly RAF fighter pilots, felt that Bomber Command should have a special campaign medal. It was possible for a man to complete a whole tour - normally calculated as 30 operations to defended targets - and receive no decoration whatsoever apart from the medal automatically given to all aircrew who completed a single operation, such as, the Air crew Europe Star.

Moreover, once the war was won, the RAF had to be drastically reduced in size. Many air crew with a log book proudly filled with operational flights were given the choice of leaving the RAF or of accepting a lower rank, such as, a Flight Lieutenant instead of a Wing Commander. NCOs who had previously held a ground trade had the choice of leaving or of being demoted to a lowly LAC or even AC2, just as if they had been court-martialed! In fact, there was no alternative to what seems at first to be a poor reward for their courage. It was in no sense punishment, but reflected the reduced opportunities available in a contracting service.

What is incontestable is that over the past fifty years, the role of Bomber Command has been repeatedly analysed and questioned on moral grounds. One veteran recently said, "At the end of the War, I was a hero; today I am a mass murderer." This is because the opinions of fresh generations are moulded by commentators who were born after 1945, and who by accident or design have overlooked many of the relevant factors.

Elements of today's media appear to prefer sensational stories of disaster or issues which can be presented as highly contentious. It is easy to argue that the daylight raid by 12 Lancasters in the MAN factory at Augsburg was a costly error, or that the famous raid on the great dams achieved little, or that the entire campaign of

Bomber Command consumed resources that might have been better applied elsewhere.

It is difficult to write with dispassionate objectivity. Even if one sticks strictly to the facts, today's media have shown how easily 'facts' can be manipulated and distorted. Despite this, it is at least possible to give a flavour of how people thought 50 years ago.

By 1941, cities throughout Europe had been bombed by the Luftwaffe, and helpless refugees machine-gunned from the air. These missions were flown with the sole objective of terrorizing the civilian population and breaking any will to resist. In 1940-42 the Luftwaffe devastated London, Coventry, Southampton, Bristol, Plymouth, Sheffield, Liverpool, Cardiff, Glasgow and many other British cities. From April, 1942, its raids on Britain were specifically directed against cities distinguished by three stars in the 'Baedeker' guidebook, as being "of historic interest."

By 1941 the United Kingdom was isolated as the only part of Europe still holding out against Hitler. Ringed by U-boats and suffering heavy air attack, it had no means of hitting back except by Bomber Command.

Bomber Command's targets were selected by the War Cabinet, who were themselves influenced by the suggestions of the Ministry of Economic Warfare. The Commander in Chief, who from 22 February, 1942, was Sir Arthur Harris, could not dictate policy (though he could offer advice). His duty was to assign targets and units to carry out the orders given to him.

Nobody can reduce to tidy arithmetic the overall effect of the devastation of Germany, nor what might have been done had the same effort been applied to some other method of waging war (but what?). Common sense surely tells us that, without sustained attacks on Hitler's war machine, D-Day could not have taken place in 1944, or if it had, it might have been a costly failure. In any case without Bomber

Command and the equally courageous daytime attacks by the US 8th Army Air Force, it is difficult to imagine what could have been a viable alternative.

In the United States it is still fashionable to show respect to the flag and honour America's heroes. In Britain it seems more fashionable to pick on people previously loved and venerated and by subtle propaganda show that they were evil schemers, incompetent fools, weak dupes or in any other way unworthy of respect. This is for the sole reason that the media are competitive, and headlines are made by scandal, failure and controversy.

Today morality of bombing cities is a favourite media subject. What is less easy to explain is why the debate has centred exclusively upon RAF Bomber Command. The media appear to forgotten the flattening by the Luftwaffe of Guernicia in Spain, Warsaw, Rotterdam, Belgrade, Stalingrad, Leningrad, or the cities of Great Britain. The totally random assaults on the civil populations by Hitler's flying bombs have faded into history. The fire raids by the US Army Air Force on Tokyo, killing far more people than any other air attacks in history, are likewise forgotten, except by the Japanese.

Yet millions of people around the world know that in February, 1945, Bomber Command made a devastating attack on the city of Dresden. This was portrayed as a wicked act, ordered entirely by Harris. What actually happened was quite different.

In late January 1945, before he left for a conference of the Allied leaders at Yalta in the USSR, Prime Minister Churchill asked what evidence he could offer Stalin of Western air support. His Secretary of State for Air, Sir Archibald Sinclair, replied "Opportunities might be used to exploit the situation by the bombing of large cities in eastern Germany, such as Leipzig, Dresden and Chemnitz, which are not only administrative centres but also the main communication centres." Churchill replied "I asked whether large cities in east Germany should not now be considered especially attractive targets. I am glad that this is under examination. Pray report to me tomorrow what is going to be done."

On the 27th of January, Harris received formal instructions... "as soon as the moon and weather conditions allow, you will undertake to attack Dresden, Leipzig, Chemnitz or any cities where a severe blitz can be carried out." Harris was against this, pointing out the great distance involved and the small advantage to be gained for what he thought would be severe casualties. He was overruled. Against his will he sent 804 bombers to Dresden on the night of 13 February. Next morning the US 8th Air Force attacked Dresden. Harris attacked Chemnitz that night, but the following morning, 15th February, the 8th Air Force attacked Dresden again. The 8th Air Force made further heavy attacks on Dresden on 2 March and 7 April, but the belief implanted in the mind of today's populations is that Dresden was wantonly destroyed by the RAF alone to satisfy Harris's lust for victims.

Harris was the last man to attempt to offer excuses or justifications. Perhaps he realised he was being made the scapegoat for any future condemnations. He may also have wondered if after his death, a statue would be erected to him which would promptly be daubed with red paint by ignorant protesters. He would have said, "Sometimes I argued, as at Dresden, but when I received a direct order I always carried it out with good grace."

Anger aroused in Britain today by this attack would have seemed utterly incomprehensible to the British population 50 years ago. Churchill struck the mood of the time when on 14 July 1941, he said, "It is time that the German should be made to suffer in their own homeland and cities something of the torment they have twice in our lifetime let loose upon their neighbours and upon the world."

Today few people have any idea of the tremendous role played by Bomber Command in winning the war. How many know that it destroyed the majority of huge barges, in which Hitler expected to bring his armies to invade Britain— losing 718 aircrew, compared with 497 by Fighter Command – so that even if the Battle of Britain had been lost, a successful invasion would almost certainly have been impossible? Without any public adulation, Bomber Command then sank seven of Hitler's 15 major warships, annihilated his merchant fleet and destroyed or 'contracepted' hundreds of his U Boats.

Hitler's production czar, Albert Speer, said, " The bombing of Germany deprived the German forces of 75 per cent of their heavy anti-tank guns, because these 88 mm guns had to be used as anti-aircraft guns, scattered all over Germany because we never knew where the bombers would strike next. Field Marshal Milch had 90,000 fit soldiers manning those guns. In addition, hundreds of thousands of expert tradesmen could not be called up into the Army because their skills were needed to repair bomb damage." Dr. Horst Boog, Chief Historian in the Military Office in Freiburg, notes that "the aluminium in the fuses of the flack shells would have built 40,000 additional fighter aircraft."

Nobody can say how many British lives were saved by the attack on the rocket laboratory at Peenemunde, and on the rocket and the flying bomb transport network and launch sites, but it must be many thousands. When the Allied armies were well established in France after D-Day, Field Marshall Rommel said "Stop the bombers or we can't win!" Nobody can say how many British soldiers were saved by bombing Le Havre; the city was taken – giving the Allies their first Channel port at the cost of 30 British troops, whilst rounding up 11,000 demoralised Germans. Bombers stopped Sepp Dietrich's armour in the Ardennes (the Battle of the Bulge) by cutting all his supply routes; General Dietrich said, "Not even the best troops in the world can stand up to this heavy bombing."

Repeatedly, whenever the Allied armies were held up by stubborn resistance, Bomber Command was always on call to eliminate the opposition. Their culminating achievement in such an operation was to allow the British Army to cross the Rhine at Wesel with just 36 casualties instead of the thousands which had been expected.

Yet, once it was clear that victory was in sight, the decision was taken apparently at the highest level in the British Government to distance itself from the strategic bombing campaign carried out by Harris under its own 'ministers'' orders. It seems that, with hindsight, the politicians saw that Bomber Command's destruction of Germany might later prove an embarrassment, and therefore it would be convenient for its collective bravery, dedication and sacrifice to be unrecognised and unrewarded.

This extraordinary ingratitude to some of the nation's bravest men was bad enough, but in recent years it has become fashionable for historians to denigrate their efforts and their leader. The reason is that, over 50 years, the public perception of bombing of cities has undergone a U-turn. In World War 2 it was an accepted and obvious way to hit back at the enemy. Today, as these words are written, the Russian Airforce is bombing the city of Grozny, and the world is united in its condemnation. This is why *So Many* has been created, to tell in a simple and direct way the stories of the men who took part in World War 2 half a century ago, when attitudes were totally different.

Today's media naturally reflect the change in public opinion, but does not excuse a rewriting of history. This has caused distress to those who actually made it, and in 1992 the problem became particularly acute in Canada. Canada's contribution to Bomber Command has been enormous, in training air crew, and in building Hampdens, Lancasters and Mosquitoes. Canadians have a right to feel proud of the giant role their country played in winning the War, but now, as one veteran put it, "We are made to appear as moronic mass-murderers and nut cases."

Canadian veterans were so incensed by what they saw as a gross and deliberate misrepresentation of their war role that they resorted to legal action in an attempt to restore at least a vestige of truth. Hurtful though all this has been to those who suffered and survived, they find it a comfort to see that those who chose to hold opinions contrary to true history are nevertheless free to broadcast those opinions.

They are able to do this because 55,573 men of Bomber Command gave their lives in order that future generations should not be slaves under the Swastika but enjoy such freedom. We owe it to them to preserve a record of what they really did, and what they really thought and felt, and what kind of people they really were.

B.G.

ISBN 1-4120-0099-8